CALLED

Air Force Chaplain, Colonel, Minister and Family Man

DAVID MARKWALDER

Thank you, family, for encouraging me while I was in a dark wilderness for five long years. This memoir would not have been possible if God had not completely healed me from hydrocephalus (water on the brain). After seeing four neurologists and two neurosurgeons, and going from a healthy jogger to shuffling, I had brain surgery at Mayo Clinic in Phoenix, Arizona on September 20, 2021. To God be the Glory!

Acknowledgements

I want to thank my wife, Marsha, for encouraging me to put this memoir together and giving up hours of valuable time together. Your patience and proofreading the many pages were amazing and deeply appreciated. Excellent suggestions from other family members were also valuable.

Contents

Air Force Chaplain, Colonel, Minister and Family Man

My Life When Growing Up

Growing Up with two sisters: One older by two years, Carol Bussell, who lives in Cambridge, Maryland and one younger, Florence Jordan, four years younger, who moved from Porterville, CA to Wisconsin in 2018. Being raised in a three bedroom home with only one bathroom made it a challenge at times. The girls shared a bedroom next to the bathroom, and I had a bedroom in the den which had two doors, one to the kitchen and one to the front hall, so much for privacy. I had a small little bed that pulled out into a double bed which was seldom used. I remember the mailbox slot at the foot of my bed where the mail was delivered.

Dad worked at Continental Can Company (3 Cs) as a plant accountant, got up every morning at 6:30 am, and left for work at 7:30 am in his reliable 1949 Chevrolet. It was a 6-cylinder, dark green stick shift that I learned how to drive on. Dad would drive to 3 Cs which was four miles away, towards downtown San Jose as a Plant Accountant for 35 years. He was like clockwork and faithfully provided for his family.

Once a year in the summer, Dad would get a 2-week vacation in which the family would go camping in Tuolumne Meadows above Yosemite National Park. Since the elevation was 10,000 feet high, it was very cold in the early morning. All five of us slept in a pop-up tent. Dad had a fishing buddy, Pat Phay, who also had a pop-up tent. So every morning they would get up at the crack of dawn and drive for an hour towards one of the lakes in the high sierras. Park at a trailhead, hike for another 3-4 miles to a pristine lake with no one else there, and fish all day.

As a young boy, patience was not one of my virtues growing up. So Danny Phay and I would go hiking or find something else to do besides fishing. Once we found a raft and played with it all afternoon, pretending we were Mark Twain and Tom Sawyer. It was a good time. We became close friends and even sang together in harmony when we were teenagers. Unfortunately, he had a wild streak in him so his parents never trusted him. I really liked him and felt sorry for him. He was very gifted but never developed his potential.

Every weekend, our family would drive over to Santa Cruz, a 30-mile trip over the mountains, to visit my dad's parents. They had six small plots of land in which they grew a thriving garden of fruits and vegetables. They even raised enough grapes to make several quarts of pure grape juice. It was very tasty and delicious. My grandpa, Adolf, painted homes part-time and my grandmother raised the garden and chickens. They had a chicken coup with around 20 chickens which laid eggs for them to eat. My grandmother, Emma, was a hard worker and a great chef. We always had large meals and the kitchen was the hub. She loved to cook and feed her family. She wore a straw hat and high-top black tennis shoes. Their house was very small with only three rooms and an indoor porch but they were happy. They went to the Assembly of God church every Sunday and Wednesday night. They also provided grape juice for communion for their church each month.

After Grandpa Markwalder died at 86, Grandma Markwalder would walk to church three miles away. They were very hearty people who loved life. They lived six blocks from the Boardwalk and beaches so I always enjoyed visiting them. Its amazing how little they had but how happy they were. They had a strong faith in God. I remember Grandpa getting up every morning early and praying for his family. He even prayed that I would become a minister. So I guess my path was cut out early on.

I remember every Thursday night my mother would drop us kids off at her mother's house in downtown San Jose and then go to her Women's Missionary Council meeting at the church. She was the president of this organization for 20+ years. Not sure where Dad was but I guess he was working overtime. At Grandma Rudine, we played with her dominoes and watched the Lone Ranger on black and white television. If I had free time, I would go climbing up the indoor stairs that went to the two apartments they rented out. I loved sliding down the large banister and climbing on the outside of the stairs and banister. Whenever I got caught, I received a lecture of how dangerous it was. But as a typical child, I felt totally safe.

That reminds me of climbing the large oak tree in our backyard. I felt totally safe as I climbed to see how high I could get. This did not make many points with my father, who would always say you're going to fall down and hurt yourself. But back then, I had no fear of heights and would continue to do it whenever Dad was gone. There was just something thrilling about pushing the envelope.

Christmas Week

Thank you, God, for loving us so much that you sent Jesus into the world to bring us new hope and a plan to restore our relationship with you. In the beginning, everything was perfect, and there was no sin in this world, but humans disobeyed you and violated your plan for us. Humans since then have gone on their own direction thinking they have a better way and making themselves gods. So God changed His plan and sent Jesus into our world to give us hope and forgiveness for our sins.

As a child, I remember we would read the Christmas story from the Bible before opening up any gifts. This was a very important tradition. We would get together with the Hammonds and grandpa and grandma Markwalder either at the Hammond's home in Lakeport or our home in San Jose.

With all these people, you can imagine all the presents there would be.

One of my favorite gifts was an electric football game with a board and 22 players. I had a lot of fun pretending two different teams played against each other. Although we lived a very modest life, mom and dad were very generous with giving us gifts at Christmas.

Tennis in High School

My high school was 10th-12th grades only. In my sophomore year, I went out for the varsity tennis team and got to play in the 8th place, which meant I played doubles. The first five positions were singles and the next four positions played doubles. I felt blessed just to make the team, as many seniors were excellent tennis players. Although we were at the bottom of the players, we won most of our matches and did our part to help have a winning tennis team.

The coach of our tennis team was an older man who was the teacher of the metal shop. He was a respectable coach who raised a winning team. When the seniors graduated, it was almost like starting over again, except that the #1 player was a junior and son of a state legislator. He came from a well-to-do family who lived on University Ave and eventually went to the University of California in Santa Barbara. My junior year in high school, I moved up to play in the #3 position and we had a fair tennis team because we lost so many senior starters.

In my senior year, the gentleman who had been our tennis coach for years retired and Abraham Lincoln High School hired a new coach who was a young man in his 20s who was a professional tennis player at the San Jose Swim and Racquet Club. I remember when I first met him; he drove up in a sports car next to the tennis courts and introduced himself. WOW! We were blessed to have him as our coach. He had short blond hair and was about 6' tall with a good build. He met with us every day after school to help us improve our skills as tennis players. I was fortunate and moved up to be the #1 player for our team. I was fast on my feet and was a natural athlete, and loved this game. Although I never had one tennis lesson, it came to me naturally and I excelled in this sport. Because I was 6' tall and slender, I had a strong serve and could get to the net quickly to put the point away. Our new coach took an interest in me and improved my game in my senior year. Our tennis team did really well and took first place in San Jose.

I remember playing the #1 tennis player at Pioneer High School in Almaden on a Saturday morning at San Jose State University to determine the top tennis player in San Jose after a week-long tennis tournament. He was from a wealthy family and had several years of tennis lessons. He was a very confident player and the match lasted two hours and went three sets. It was a very close game, and I almost beat him.

Our new tennis coach wanted me to travel the tennis circuit after high school and become a professional tennis player. Unfortunately, in 1965, the Vietnam War was a major part of society and the draft was something every 18-year-old faced, especially if you had a low number. When I turned 18 on Nov 11, 1965, my draft # was 17. To avoid the draft of an unjust war, I decided to attend college and get a 2S deferment. I applied to the University of California at Santa Barbara, San Jose State University, and the University of California at Santa Cruz. They all had strong engineering departments and I was accepted to all three of the schools because I had a very good GPA of 3.8. I ended up choosing to attend San Jose State University and stay home, which was cheaper for my parents and I could stay close with Marsha and many friends. I ended up playing tennis in my freshman and sophomore years at San Jose State University.

I remember my first impression of attending college was that it was huge. There were over 30,000 students and it felt very impersonal. This was a major adjustment after attending a high school of 1500 students. My faith was tested as one of the professors who taught biology was an atheist and believed in evolutionism and Darwinism. My best friend at the time was an agnostic and brilliant student in engineering. Russ Ingram and I clicked and I respected him as a person. He had Christian values, though he was not a Christian.

He married a Japanese gal, Patty, and had a Buddhist wedding that I was in. Life certainly took a change after high school. Fortunately, I was still attending Bethel Assembly of God Church and was dating Marsha, which kept me grounded in the faith. We used to play violin duets for the Sunday evening services and they introduced us as Marsha and David Markwalder so people thought we were sister and brother. It wasn't until we got married that it got straightened out.

Walti Hot Springs Ranch— August 1964

Walti Hot springs Ranch, 3000 acres, 100 miles south of Elko, NV and 50 miles north of Austin, NV. It was located in the middle of the desert and very hot in the summer. I worked as a ranch hand in the summers of 1964 and 1965 when I was 16 and 17. It was a great summer job and I learned the definition of hard work. I would go by Greyhound bus for 500 miles from my home in San Jose, CA and be picked up by my uncle Emil in Nevada.

Our daily routine on the ranch was getting up every morning at 5:30 am and working outside irrigating the hay field with plentiful hot water. But because the water was hot, it could burn the hay so my two uncles and I had to walk down every row to make sure it was not flooding the area. This would take an hour in the early morning and an hour in the evening when we changed it to another area. One of the joys of the evening job was there many mosquitoes just waiting to suck my blood as a city slicker and give me large bites that would itch. I remember my first two weeks counting 15-20 bites on each arm. And this was with the long-sleeved shirt that I wore.

Then, there were the large horse flies that found a perfect landing on my back between my shoulder blades when riding my horse. Each week, we would go horseback riding all day to move the cattle from one water hole to another one. Those horse flies knew exactly where to attack you where you could not swat them. Their bites really hurt and would flare up later on.

Going back to our daily routine on the ranch, after we finished irrigating the hay field, it was time to enjoy a large breakfast. This was not just a bowl of cereal but steak and eggs, potatoes or large pancakes and eggs. There was homemade applesauce at every meal. Their neighbors had an apple orchard and shared their apples. There was always plenty of milk to drink with the meal. Sometimes, the cows would eat wild hay and the milk had a very stout taste to it, which was not pleasant.

Sometimes, a mouse would find its way to the cooler and drown in the milk. There was no refrigerator because of the lack of electricity. It was a very primitive way of keeping things cool, but it worked.

Then, after breakfast, it was time to go out in the hayfield and pick up the bales of hay that had been cut and bundled. To accomplish this feat, they used a tractor that pulled a flatbed trailer with an elevator attached to one side that would scoop up the hay bales and bring them up to the flatbed where I would be standing and lift off the hay bail and stack it on the wagon. We would get an average of 100 bales of hay for each load.

When the wagon was full, we would take it into the hay yard and stack it with the other large bundles of hay. In between rounds we would always stop and get a cold drink of water from the gallon jug that we brought with us. It was covered with a gunny sack material to keep the water cool. This was our morning work before lunch. It was time to wash our hands and face outside in a basin of clean water. That always felt good and refreshing.

For lunch, there was applesauce, milk, sandwiches, salad, and pasta—noodles with a sauce. Then, we had a 30-minute break to relax before heading out to the hayfield for round two of fun. This time all three of us had a different assignment. Uncle Bill was in charge of cutting the hay. After it lay down on one side for 24 hours, I drove a tractor and a rake to put the hay in rows and help it dry on the other side. I got pretty good at making up the hay in neat rows in preparation for the third tractor to scoop it up and produce bales of hay. The challenge of my job was the wind, which at times would come up and destroy my beautiful job and scatter the hay. Then, I would have to come back the next day and do it all over again. I remember being so angry I yelled at the wind and wanted to quit. But the next day was a new start and it felt good to have this job and enjoy God's beautiful creation.

After we had each finished our assignment of cutting, raking and baling the hay, it was time for dinner. This was a big meal with steak and potatoes as we were famished for the hard physical labor we had done. There is something very satisfying about working hard and accomplishing your job. It was great physical exercise and you felt good about putting a full day of hard work in. Something about working outside and breathing in clean air that is healthy. Good, wholesome exercise is good for the body and the soul.

After dinner, there was one more piece of our workload. We needed to go outside once again and change the hot water to a new area for irrigation. Yes, this meant we needed to spend about an hour going down the rows with our shovel to make sure the water would not flood any one area and burn it. Unlike the early morning hours, it was s starting to get dark and the mosquitoes were plentiful and loved sucking the blood from a city slicker. Fortunately, my system got immune to these pesty misquotes within two weeks and I was no longer bothered by them.

If it wasn't too late, it was time to take a dip in the healing warm waters and soak all your soreness out. They had two pools with sandy bottoms. One was hot and would get up to 110 degrees as you got close to the source of the hot springs. The other one was connected to the hot pool but much cooler. That one you could swim in. Both of these ponds were pretty small, being about 30 ft. in diameter. But they were gifts to this ranch and provided healing for your body after a long day of work. They had built two small changing rooms next to the ponds.

One of the interesting facts is two large alligators were found next to these ponds several years ago. Now, only their skeletons remained. It is believed that they were dropped off there by a caravan passing through.

Now, it was time to dry off and go to bed. The sun was down and there were no lights or electricity so we would go to bed at 8:30-9:00 pm. This was normally after sitting on the back porch and enjoying a beautiful sunset against the scenic mountain. If you looked really close you might see Mustangs up on the high hill above us. This was up 3000 feet and 2-3 miles away. Always a joy when you would spot them up on the range, often running and playing. I always wanted to saddle my horse and chase them but unfortunately, that never happened.

I slept in a small room that was a walk-through with a very small bed but it was adequate. In the middle of the night, I had some unexpected visitors that woke me up. I heard these mice running along the linoleum floor, waking me up from a deep sleep. This became a nightly occurrence for my entertainment. It doesn't get any better than this, with even God's small creatures welcoming me to the ranch.

Now it was morning and time to "rise and shine." The sun was up and so was I. I jumped out of bed and put on my stiff blue jeans as they were standing up in the corner. No need to wash them as they will get dirty and sweaty again. I was told the sign of a true cowboy as if he had his pants stood up in the corner of his bedroom. I guess I passed that test. So I jumped in my blue jeans and threw a shirt on. I was ready for a new day.

The freshly cooked bacon and eggs aroma was an excellent motive to get up and greet the kitchen crew. It was Uncle Emil who was sharing his culinary skills. There wasn't anything that he could not do with only one arm. Several years ago, when he was using one of the old hay baling machines, there was a serious accident. Unfortunately, Emil's right hand and arm got pulled into the machine. By the time they were able to stop it, his right hand and forearm had got mangled and there was no way to save them. I can't imagine the pain he endured.

So he went to a doctor in San Jose, CA and stayed with us while getting fitted for a new mechanical arm that could open and close his hook by the use of his arm. He could use this device to eat, throw bales of hay, and lead a horse to corral the cows. Emil had a positive attitude in spite of his handicap. You would never know he had a problem, as that did not exist in his vocabulary. He was a joy to be around and a hard worker.

I remember once a month, Emil and I would get in the pick-up truck along with six 50-gallon barrels to fill up with gasoline. This was critical to run the tractors and work the land. The closest town was Elko, NV, which was 100 miles north over 50 miles of dirt roads. This was a monthly ritual critical for groceries, ranch equipment, and other essentials. The trip was three hours each way. It was good to see new scenery and meet other people. It was a pretty trip as we passed several of their neighbor's ranches. The Waltis had 3000 acres to raise their 1000 head of cattle. Some of these ranches had over 3000 cattle and hundreds of acres.

One of the ranches even had a private landing strip on it with a private plane. We are talking about hundreds of acres and many ranch hands to carry out the tasks. The owner was very wealthy and enjoyed the ranch to get out of the city "hum-drum and stress. But even the rich people had no wealthy stigma about them but were seen as just plain folks. You would never know they had great wealth. They shopped with the common folks and treated everyone with respect.

Another tradition of the Walti Hot Springs Ranch is turning on a generator once a week on Thursday nights. Why Thursday nights? Not sure but it was a tradition. So, on Thursday nights we got to use the lights to read the newspaper and magazines and other correspondence. This was a unique part of the weekly schedule as all other nights we went to bed at 8:30-9:00 pm when the sun went down. This was quite a treat to stay up and enjoy life. Of course, we still got up at 5:30 am when the sun came up to go work in the hay fields. This was a very healthy life style of living. Early to bed and early to rise make one healthy and wise.

Each Friday we had the unique opportunity to move the cattle from one water hole to another one several miles away. This involved saddling up and riding a horse for four hours. As a city slicker, I was pleasantly surprised by this routine. However, it quickly lost its charm after sitting in the saddle for 4+ hours. The first day I remember after two hours, I got off my horse and walked him. The horse looked at me like what is your problem. But I knew I would be plenty sore that evening. Once I got used to riding long distances I not only enjoyed the horseback ride but learned how to rope a calf with a quick-release knot. That added joy and challenge to the cattle drive.

There was one time we went up in the canyons to round up the cattle to come down to the valley. This was especially challenging and required a sure-footed horse to come down the steep mountainsides. I learned a lot about trusting your horse and balancing yourself on the saddle. This was a tremendous experience I had that summer.

At the end of summer, it was time to get all the young calves branded and to put a strong rubber band around the steer's testicles to neuter them. This was a noisy time with lots of crying from the young calves and the smell of the branding iron was unforgettable. Many times, the hot branding iron caused the calves to urinate and defecate, which added to the pleasantries of the experience. By the time this was over, you were exhausted and just wanted to go in and wash up and get ready for dinner. This was all part of being a ranch hand in the desert. This was another great memory to stay with me.

Some evenings when I wasn't too tired, I would borrow their jeep pickup and take "Shep" their sheepdog, with me for a jackrabbit hunt. This was an easy hunt as the car lights would paralyze the rabbits on the road and I simply pulled out my grandfather's 1898 Winchester rifle and took a shot from a distance. This rifle was quite accurate and I usually got a rabbit. Then the fun would begin and "Shep" would go and retrieve the rabbit so I could skin it. Shep ate the rabbit for dinner. Shep was a great dog and we had many special times together.

One afternoon when I was on the hay wagon waiting to pick up another bale of hay, I noticed that the next bail coming up the elevator had a snake on top of it. I quickly thought, what was I going to do? Fortunately, by the time the bail had reached me to take it off the lift and place it on the wagon, the snake had crawled off. I was glad to see that as I was quickly trying to discern if this was a poisonous snake. After catching my breath, I continued on the mission of filling up the wagon with many more bales of hay.

When you put them tightly on the wagon, it could hold 20 bales on the bottom, 10 x 2. Once the bottom row was finished, a second level was added. Then, a third, fourth and fifth layer was secured to make a total of 100 bales of hay to be taken into the hay yard and transferred onto a larger haystack. The challenge became when you had to throw the bale of hay over your head to stack it in the hay yard. Moving the hay down to the ground or sideways was not a challenge. But as you created the new haystack and had to lift the bail overhead, it quit becoming fun. This was great exercise and built muscle and cardio. Since the ranch was at 5500', I had to get in shape in a hurry coming from sea level. But I was young and open to the challenge. Although the work was hard, I enjoyed the experience and learning something new.

After we had completed that task, it was time to take a quick break and drink some refreshing cold water from the gallon container as we sat in the shade and discussed our accomplishments for the day. I appreciated their respect for the hard work and the compliments I received in this prestigious club. They both appreciated the hard work I had accomplished in bucking bales of hay. Whatever work I did was less work for them to do.

My first summer I was happy to earn $200 a month plus board and room. At the end of summer, I came home with a whopping $400 for the two months of work. But I also came home with muscles and I was in tip-top shape and tan. My second summer I got a raise and made $250 a month plus board and room. So, I came home with $500 to put in my bank account. There was nothing to spend it on, so I was very content with the payment. They mentioned when the price of beef comes back up they would remember me with a check. Of course, I had forgotten about this promise.

What was amazing is eight years later, when I was getting ready to graduate from seminary a letter came in the mail with a $3,000 check. Thanking me for all the hard work I had done on the ranch for them. I wanted to cry and told my wife that we were going to go to Europe in the summer of 1973 after graduating from graduate school. This allowed us to visit our relatives in Switzerland and then study at L'Abri Fellowship with Dr. Francis Schaffer in the Alps for two months. This was a dream that came true.

Now fast forward it many years, as a result of this money stashed in the bank. After we got married in 1968, it gave us money to purchase our first home for $20,000. This first little doll house of 888 square feet became our beautiful home. We eventually sold it for $93,000. It is amazing how a small amount of money grew into a larger amount with God's blessings.

Time With My Grandparents In Santa Cruz

Almost every weekend we would travel as a family 30 miles to Santa Cruz to visit my dad's parents, Adolph and Emma Markwalder. They owned six plots of land in the small suburb of Seaside, California. They both left their families in Switzerland and traveled separately by ship to reach their new promised land of America. Emma was a strong lady and refused to marry the man her father had picked out for her, so she was cut out of her inheritance. It was usually during the summer time that I was out of school and could visit them for 1-2 weeks.

I enjoyed going there and helping them out with picking there fruit or cultivating their land with a power tiller. I was a young buck and had the energy to burn, so I offered to come and help with their vast garden and trees. When I got back from the ranch in Nevada in 1964, I was in great shape and went and worked their land for them. In return I was given three large meals a day and enjoyed their company and the good feeling of helping them out. Good, hard labor was what I was used to doing.

When I was younger, I remember locking Grandpa in the garage from the outside. It was a simple wooden paddle you would move from vertical to horizontal. When Grandpa would go in the garage to get chicken feed I was close behind and helped secure the door from the outside. Poor grandpa would call out, "David, open this door right now." I usually ignored his request for several moments and then opened it up. It was always fun to tease him. I remember the time he had caught a fish in the ocean and then stuck it in my back pocket as a prank. That dead fish stunk and pulling it out of my pocket was gross.

So it was payback time and I got him good. Their tiny bathroom was a step up from an outhouse. It was located on the back porch and was barely big enough to turn around in it. The bathroom also had a lock on the outside of the door to keep the door closed. Whenever I caught him using the bathroom, I had a surprise for him when he tried to get out. Somehow, that vertical pad lock got twisted to the horizontal position---GOT YA Grandpa!!! I guess you might say that teasing was part of my DNA.

For lunch we had fresh grape juice grown and produced from their own garden. WOW was it good!!!! This was the pure quell. Between hard work with plenty of wholesome exercise, eating lots of fresh vegetables and eggs, and sleeping well, they had a good life and lived to be 88 and 94. Stress did not seem to be part of their vocabulary. They enjoyed the family and went to church every Sunday and often on Wednesday nights. They were wonderful people and others loved being around them. I was told when I was a boy, Grandpa Markwalder prayed I would be a minister when I grew up. Grandpa Markwalder, your prayer request was definitely answered.

Walk down Memory Lane With Marsha

It was the summer of 1964 when I first met my beautiful wife. I was 16 years old and Marsha was 15. I had worked on a 3000-acre cattle ranch with my uncles in the middle of Nevada, 100 miles south of Elko and 50 miles north of Austin, for two months. When I attended Sunday school, there was a new girl in town named Marsha with beautiful, big brown eyes and a warm smile that would melt you.

After dating for two years, Marsha and I got married on June 1, 1968, in San Jose, California, at Bethel Church. It was a Friday night and 800 people attended our wedding. Talk about getting tired of shaking everyone's hand in the receiving line. This was also Marsha's parent's 21st wedding anniversary. There was a tradition in those days to chase the bride and groom after the reception in their cars. We fortunately outsmarted all but one car and left early enough to avoid this. We drove 30 miles to Santa Cruz and stayed in the Dream Inn for our first night.

The next day, we started our journey down the coast on Highway 101 towards Disneyland. We did not have much money but we were very happy. Along the way, we ate at a steak house in Moro Bay and we must have been glowing because the owner said the dinner was on them. He might as well have given us $100 as this felt like we had hit the jackpot.

After the honeymoon we returned back to San Jose and rented a unit in a fourplex that belonged to Marsha's parents. We managed the place for them in exchange for free rent. What a great deal this was for us newlyweds. Marsha had a full-time job at Cristina Warehouse, where she was the inventory control clerk. While Marsha worked full-time, I still had two more years of college to get my bachelor's degree. In addition to my studies, I worked part-time as a draftsman and I was a bag boy for a grocery store every Saturday. It is amazing how fussy some ladies could be with how they wanted their groceries bagged. Those were also the ones who would give you the lowest tips.

After a year of living in the fourplex, Marsha's mother, Helena, helped us buy our first home at 484 McCamish in south San Jose, close to IBM. I had saved $2,000 in my bank account for the down payment and we paid a whopping $20,000 for a little 2-bedroom bath doll house with 888 square feet. It was perfect for us and there was plenty of work to be done, like adding a sprinkler system and designing the front yard with a low decorative brick fence and rock concrete steps descending down to the sidewalk. We worked very hard finishing this home and Marsha would remind me, "None of your other girlfriends would have done this." I replied, "That's why I married you."

On the inside, we added a valance over the kitchen windows along with window coverings in all the rooms. This was our first home and we loved it—small but cozy. When we moved to Pasadena, CA, in 1970, where I attended graduate school at Fuller Theological Seminary, we rented our home out to pay for the monthly mortgage. The first tenant was a single lady with two daughters. She was an excellent tenant whom we had for several years. Unfortunately, we had other tenants who were not good. Being an absentee landlord is not the best way to take care of business. In 1982, we sold it for a nice profit. This was our first taste of real estate.

An Athletic Girlfriend

One of the things I prided myself on was my athletic ability. Whether talking about football, basketball, tennis, or just running, I sought to do my best and excel. That is probably one of the reasons I found Marsha Garcia appealing to date. She was very athletic and good at various sports like basketball, tennis, and track. She would stretch out her legs before and after running and became quite flexible.

It was a big embarrassment for me when I challenged her to a kicking above-the-head contest that took place in the alleyway of my grandparents' home in Santa Cruz. She first did a kick to show me how high she could do it and I was very impressed. Now it was my turn and not to be outdone, I kicked my right leg so high I ended up landing on the ground. I was not about to be shown up but I was and had to eat my pride. I quickly learned that I was not as flexible as my girlfriend. I had to learn a lesson the hard way.

Keith Family

When we were at Knox Presbyterian Church in 1971 as a youth director, we met several fabulous people in this church. One of our gifts of friendship was a single gentleman named Chuck Keith. He was an insurance man at the time and volunteered to help us with our youth group. Chuck assisted Marsha in teaching the junior high Sunday school class and also went with us on winter camps at Forest Home. Chuck was very organized and was a great asset as an adult leader for our youth. This was the beginning of a very long and solid friendship.

Chuck was dating Dominique, a single French lady whom he met on a foreign exchange trip that led to a long romance. Domie soon moved from France and was married to Chuck and we became best friends with her too. Before children, we often had several dinners together and played double-handed Pinnacle for fun. I remember one dinner when Chuck asked if he could say grace and announced through the prayer that Domie was pregnant with Eric. We also ate a whole Sarah Lee pie for dessert as Chuck quartered it for us.

Once our families grew, we celebrated Thanksgiving and Easter together. Thanksgiving was Uncle Chuck's favorite holiday, so we celebrated it at their home in Lake Forest and there was always plenty of food. Chuck loved to cook and outdid himself at Thanksgiving time with lots of Turkey, stuffing, mashed potatoes and all the other fixings. Another tradition with the Keith's was to enjoy a Pinacolada before any meal at the Keith's home. They tasted so good and were a great way to begin a time of special fellowship with them. During our time together, our children would create and perform a unique play for us to enjoy. Jewel was the director of the play and always got to do the leading role which was brilliant on her part. We loved to see our children play to gather. There were five of them: Keith's Eric and Chantal, and Markwalder's Jewel, Star, and Chanelle. Our kids enjoyed playing and growing up together.

Another vacation was when they drove from Lake Forest, California to Colorado Springs, Colorado, to go white water rapids with us. We stayed overnight next to the river. The ladies stayed in our motorhome and Chuck, Eric and I stayed on the floor of Indian Tepees that were at the campsite. The next day, it was time to have fun on the rapids. This was a highlight of the day as we got in a water fight with neighboring rafters. Another distinct thing that happened was when Chuck almost fell out of the raft and Domie grabbed him to pull him back in. We also enjoyed riding through some very rough rapids that got all of us wet. It was a thrill to make it through some glaring rough waters without any incident or loss. Chuck had a good sense of humor and one time hollered out an Indian chant at the other rafters and lifted his oar saying, "Callimunga."

We had the privilege of celebrating weddings and baptisms together. Eric and Chantal flew out to Colorado to attend Jewel and Christian's wedding in 1998. When Eric got married, we traveled out to California to celebrate this happy occasion. A few years later, they asked me to officiate at Chantal and Justin's wedding in December. It was an outdoor wedding and was extremely cold. I was glad I was wearing my heaving black robe but felt sorry for the bridal party and bride who wore dresses and were freezing. Uncle Chuck gave Chantal away and as a typical educator, took notes on his hand of the wedding service.

Unfortunately, Chuck died way too early in December 2006, right after I retired from the Air Force in October. He missed our other two daughters' wedding: Chanelle in September 2012 in Bishop, California and Starlene's wedding in May 2021 at the Arrowhead Golf Course in Denver. But Domie and all her children and grandchildren came to celebrate with us. Whenever we meet with the Keiths, there is a big hole because Chuck is no longer with us. When you have someone as special as Uncle Chuck, you do not replace him. The only good news is we look forward to seeing him again in heaven.

Houseboat Trip at Knox Presbyterian Church

One year after I became the part-time youth director for Knox Presbyterian Church in Los Angeles, we wanted to send our youth group to a summer camp like Forest Home. Our young people were so liberal they said "no"—that's where all the Jesus freaks go!! Then, they handed me an ad for a houseboat trip in the Sacramento Delta. This was 400 miles away and there were no chaperones to work with us. Finally, we presented it to the Elders to see if they would buy it. To our surprise, they said yes to a 7-day and 6-night journey once on the water.

Mary Ann Miguel, who had two sons in our youth group, volunteered for us to use her station wagon. Piece by piece this trip came together. I was only 24 and Marsha 23 when this trip took place. We were responsible for 12 young people 15-18 years of age. We knew this was the only way to win these young people, so we did it. We traveled 400 miles each way just to get there. Then, there was the responsibility of chartering a 30' houseboat and driving it on the fingers of the Sacramento Delta. Looking back, I thought, "What were we thinking?" That was a lot of pressure put on a young husband and wife. But it was the right decision and it led to many good Bible studies in the morning, outstanding free time to discuss the resurrection of Jesus on the roof of the houseboat in the afternoon, and just let the Spirit work its freedom with these liberal teens.

We set out with a few important rules for the teens to agree to: no alcohol, no drugs, no sex and respect your leaders. Any violation would result in an automatic one-way bus ticket home. It was the wisest thing we could have done. We had no problems with these youth although they had done everything in the book. There was a mutual respect and God's Spirit reigned. It was a great joy to witness these young people get turned on by Bible stories and ask deep questions about their faith.

As a result many of them became Christians over the next several months. This became an exciting time for our youth group. We followed this up with a water ski trip to Lake Elsenor at Bill and Ruth Schoelerman's cabin. This was another spiritual turning point for many of our teens. After this, they were ready to attend a snow camp at Forest Home, which they would not do before now. It was a joy to witness God's Spirit move in this powerful way.

Trip to Europe in 1973

I had just graduated from Fuller Theological Seminary in June 1973. Now, it was time to move on with our lives and not look back. I had successfully completed my Master of Divinity degree after three challenging years of graduate school. In order to not add any debt to our marriage, I worked two part time jobs during my final two years. I was a youth director at Knox Presbyterian Church in LA next to the International Airport for 20-25 hours a week. The second job, I worked as a teacher/coach for a Children's Development Center from 2-6 pm after school each day. I was both a teacher and coach for the center. I worked with four other female teachers and taught approximately 50-grade school children at an after-school program. We directed arts and crafts, outdoor sports, and a reading program for the children. During this time, Marsha worked full-time at a furniture store and part-time with me at Knox Pres.

In addition to these two part-time jobs, I was a full-time graduate student taking 15-18 units a quarter. Because of my two jobs, I graduated with only a $1500 loan. In addition, I received a $3000 check from my summer job I had done for two summers on the Walti Hot Springs Ranch in Nevada. My uncles had told me that when the price of beef gets better they would send me a check to help make up for the lack of pay in 1964-1965. I had completely forgotten about their promise when a check for $3000 came in the mail the spring of 1973. I accepted it as a God wink, saying well done.

So we decided to plan a 3-month trip to Europe and visit our Swiss relatives, L'Abri Fellowship, for two months, followed by a 3-week whirlwind train trip through Switzerland,

Germany, Italy, Holland, Austria and France. This was a whirlwind trip visiting museums, concerts, eating many wonderful meals, and sightseeing to our hearts content. We both commented it is a good thing we are doing this while we are young.

We not only faced constant language changes as we went from country to country, having to find a new hotel to stay at, and had to change our currency every few days. Talk about getting out of your comfort zone. But we did it and really enjoyed all the new people we got to meet and learn about their lives. In Austria we even stayed at a bed and breakfast and had a yummy breakfast. This was truly a trip of a lifetime. We also did a lot of hitchhiking in Europe and felt very safe. It was a great way to meet new people and save money.

I look back now and say I can't believe we did that but we were young and adventuresome. Fortunately, we did not have one bad experience. I can remember getting picked up on this dark and winding road that went up to our chalet. After several minutes, a young Swiss man picked us up and drove up the road that was part of a Grand Prix raceway. We latter found out he was a race driver and enjoyed driving on all the switchbacks that he encountered. The one good piece of advice I received before this trip was never put the lady in the back seat. This was a precaution to prevent someone from driving off with your lady.

1956 Morgan Plus 4

In 1975, after graduating from Fuller Theological Seminary, I decided to trade my 1968 Datsun 2000 sports car for my cousin's 1956 Morgan Plus four sports car. I had always loved this sports car, which Bill and Winnie Becker had owned since it was new. They had beefed up the engine and won many races with it because it could out-corner almost all cars including Porches. It was a true sports car with no heater or windows and had a long louvre front end and was handmade in England by Peter Morgan company. It was the only car that had a wooden frame which increased its ability to be flexible and corner very well.

It had a small, little jump seat in the back and Winnie had kept two small furniture benches that fit perfectly for two small riders. When the twins were small, I would put them back there and Jewel in the front for a ride around the neighborhood. I remember taking them up on Woodman in Colorado Springs before all the homes got built there. We had lots of fun and that was before seat belts were mandatory.

I purchased the Morgan for $2000 from the Beckers and sold the Datsun for the same price. We used to love to visit Bill and Winnie on Saturdays when I was in seminary. They lived in Woodman Hills, 30 miles from where we lived in Pasadena, CA. When it was hot, we loved to go swimming in their pool in their backyard, which was very refreshing. They always cooked us a rich dinner like BBQ chicken with garlic French bread that was soaked in butter. You were guaranteed to have heartburn from this high-cholesterol meal. But it sure was delicious. We always enjoyed our time with Bill and Winnie and their two boys, Dane Morgan and Todd. Bill was an avid reader and had a new book going, while Winnie was the jokester and was loaded with funny stories. She loved to embarrass us and one time, we went to the grocery store to pick up some food when she ran into some friends from church. She said, "I usually don't shop on Sundays, but I have some guests drop in." What was funny is her friends were shopping too so why be embarrassed.

I spent many hours restoring that car in Harold Perong's mother's garage, who was an elder at Knox Presbyterian Church when I was a youth pastor and his son was in our youth group. It was people's generosity that allowed me to store the Morgan in a garage to strip it down and build it back up. I added two Webber carburetors to replace the SU ones on there. The Webbers were more efficient and gave it more horsepower. It now had 150 horsepower and only weighed 1800 pounds. It had a Jaguar moss gearbox for transmission and could really move out. I remember racing my friend's Datsun 240Z, which was the hottest sports car on the market and beat it hands down.

After adding the Webber carburetors on the Morgan, I needed to have a special scoop created on the same side to give them plenty of air. When all the bodywork was completed, I then changed the original color, which was all black, to a beautiful two-tone silver and black. It was a real head-turner as there were very few Morgans on the road. It looked like an old MG but had a longer hood in front.

My only complaint about the Morgan is it was not a reliable car and would often break down and need to be fixed especially in the cold weather of Colorado. Unfortunately, you had to order most of the replacement parts from England, which would take forever. So I decided in 1988, when we lived in San Bernardino, CA to sell the Morgan after giving my cousin Winnie the first choice to buy it back. She was not interested in purchasing it but did offer to help sell it and put an ad in the Los Angeles Times for me. What happened next was an absolute miracle. In less than one week, she had a full offer for $15,000 from a rich father in Malibu CA. He bought it for his son as a graduation present from high school. His only request was to drive it up his steep driveway to his home which overlooked the Pacific Ocean. So Winnie drove it one last time and I was the co-pilot as we slowly crawled up the steep driveway. Then we had a steak dinner and shared all about the history of the Morgan.

Lessons in Karate

As a young man, I was fascinated with the art of Karate. During my time as a youth pastor in Los Angeles, I signed up to take Karate lessons in the evening as part of my physical exercise. I was in my twenties and I discovered that Karate was both physically and mentally challenging. I took a form of Karate called Tang Soo Do, which is from Korea. Taking Karate is a form of physical discipline that improves your balance, strength, mental focus and stretching. The purpose of Karate is not to smash your opponent but to have the tools to prevent a fight if possible. Self-defense is its primary goal.

I spent a couple of years taking Karate in Los Angeles and was promoted to becoming a red belt, which was the level right below accomplishing a black belt. I never made it to black belt because we left Los Angeles and moved to Colorado Springs for a job change. This temporarily ended my quest to attain a Black Belt in 1981 at the age of 33 years of age.

One never knows what life may bring you and this was certainly true in my journey. In 1990, I was accepted to attend Air Command and Staff College as a Major in the Air Force at Air University in Montgomery, Alabama. This was a 10-month in Residence College, so I moved to this area and left my family in Colorado Springs. They could have moved with me but when I asked the girls if they wanted to move to Montgomery, Alabama, they said, "Dad, we love you but we are going to miss you." I took our 20' motorhome and, pulled our VW bug behind it and headed to Alabama, where I lived at the Family Camp on the Air Force base. When I arrived there, it was in August and the temperature was 90 -100 degrees with lots of humidity. Our motorhome did not have any air conditioning but only a large square fan to keep me cool. I also encountered fire ants in the middle of the night that had invaded my bed. What a great initiation I received but I knew this was where God had called me and I was fine.

Not only did I receive an excellent education on subjects that included leadership, personnel, personality traits, Space Command, conventional warfare, and various other subjects important to the Air Force. The pace of the training was very fast and I often felt like I was drinking from a fire hose. Just as you mastered one subject, it was time to move on to a new topic. It was a privilege to be among 800 of the top officers selected to attend this school. I enjoyed meeting numerous Air Force officers and becoming their friends. Being a chaplain gave me the unique opportunity to not only be a student but a minister to them. I also enjoyed many profound questions from the speakers in our large lecture hall on morality and critical issues facing us.

To stay in good physical shape while attending these classes, I went to the gym but also discovered a Tang Soo Do Karate class in the evening to attend. It's amazing this class was being taught on base at the MWR center twice a week at 6 pm. I could hardly believe that the same style of Karate that I had taken years before in Los Angeles was being offered here. What were the chances of this happening? Very slim, but it did happen. I signed up and joined the class, which allowed me to meet other Air Force personnel. Most of them were in the Security Force field, including our instructor. Rick was a 3rd-degree black belt who enjoyed having a chaplain join his ranks. He was married to Lisa, a short blond who was also in the class. There were 4-5 ladies who were taking the class.

Rick was not only an excellent karate instructor but I learned later on that he had a deep faith and played the drums for a praise team at his church. It was nice to have that common faith between us, besides our common interest in the art of Karate. When Marsha and the girls visited me for Christmas in 1990, I took them to my Karate class and introduced them to Rick. He invited them to join the class that evening and they showed great promise in their kicking technique.

After my ten months of Karate while at Air Command and Staff College, I was hired to be the head of the Professional Division at the Air Reserve Personnel Center (ARPC) in Denver, Colorado. This allowed our family to stay in Colorado Springs as I commuted to my new job in Denver. I was blessed by having several different people in my car pool who worked at ARPC. This was very critical since I commuted for 12 years. It was during this time that one of my jobs was to speak at the Chaplain School at Maxwell Air Force Base in Montgomery, Alabama. This meant I flew to the base where my former Karate class existed. Rick allowed me to join the Karate class whenever in town and practice on my own toward earning my Black Belt. Finally on July 19, 1993, I took my test for becoming a Black Belt and passed. This was a great joy for me and Rick to reach this high accomplishment.

Dave's Angels

Charlie's Angels was a popular television series in the 1970s when our three daughters were born in Los Angeles. Jewel was born in 1975 and the twins came into this world in 1977. This gave me the inspiration to call my girls "Dave's Angels." All three of them are beautiful and talented, like Charlie's Angels.

In fact, Charlie's Angels television called my wife with the offer to pick her up and the twins in a limousine, along with $1000 to have the twins on Charlie's Angels. Evidently they needed twins on the set and, due to the lighting rules, would swap them out. This happened within a week of the twin's birth. Although this was a very tempting offer, especially in light of my low youth ministry salary, Mom declined the offer because our twins were not identical in looks. I thought their looks were close enough but I lost that battle. Sorry twins, you almost became television stars before your big sister.

Starlene and Chanelle came home from the hospital on Jewel's birthday. They became her babies and everyone who came by to see the twins had a gift for Jewel too. This was an exciting time for our family. We lived in a two-bedroom condo, which got smaller with the addition of the twins. The dining room area became the residence of the twins. We had numerous babysitters from the church I worked at, including high school kids from our youth group. They fell In love with our children. This was a big blessing. We did not slow down one bit but took our girls everywhere we went. They enjoyed being a part of our youth group and were loved during the many events.

Long Train Ride to California

It was the summer of 1983 when Marsha and I decided to take a train ride from Denver, Colorado, to San Francisco, California, with our three young girls. We heard that the trip was beautiful, crossing the Rocky Mountains and the Sierra Nevada Mountains by train. It was a 33-hour trip and because of the added expense of getting a private sleeper car, we decided to only stay in a regular car. This meant we would sit up all night long. I served at First Presbyterian Church in Colorado Springs as the Minister of Single Adults and worked 70-75 hour weeks because of several evenings and weekend retreats for 1400 singles. I was in dire need of a restful vacation and this sounded like a good change from driving across the Utah and Nevada deserts to get to San Jose, California.

Although this was a solid plan, the cost of taking the train was not much more than driving our motor home and getting only ten miles per gallon of gas. We thought it would be less stressful than driving and seeing some new scenic views. Our daughters (Jewel-7, Star and Chanelle-5) would love to travel on a train for the first time and were able to get up from their seats and walk around. They would also be able to use the restroom on the train and enjoy looking out the train's large windows. All of this came into play when we made this important decision to take this train ride. As frugal as we were, we brought along food to eat on the train. All of this sounded good, right? We had done our homework and we were ready to drive to Denver to catch our 33-hour journey on the train.

Unfortunately, there was one large glitch in our dream train ride that we could not identify until the actual experience. The girls were all packed and excited to enjoy this new venture. We got to Denver and entered the large, exotic lobby to purchase our tickets. Denver has a very nostalgic train station that captures the hearts and minds of many travelers. It was a great start to our vacation. As we got on the train, it felt good to be doing something entirely different than our usual long drive of 1400 miles across two deserts to San Jose, California. We usually tried to drive to San Jose to visit both of our families twice a year. We always looked forward to seeing our parents and siblings, and it was important for our girls to see their grandparents, aunts, and uncles.

You would have thought we were on a ride in Disneyland when we got on the train. The girls were thrilled with this new experience and Marsha and I thought we made the right decision to ride the train. We didn't expect to be unable to sleep in this car with numerous children and their mothers reading out loud nursery books to them through the night. It was like being in a nursery room on steroids with no place to retreat for silence and rest. I was in dire need of rest and relaxation from my stressful job which produced much adrenalin in my body. Although the girls could sleep amid the noise, I found it impossible to turn off my mind and fall asleep. This was very frustrating for me and made it a long train ride.

If we ever decide to take the train again, we will definitely get a sleeper car for the peace and quiet it would provide. When all is said and done, we are still glad we went on the train to California. The girls had a great time and built special memories for them that can never be replaced. Sometimes mom and dad have to put the needs of their daughters first to experience a new family adventure.

Minister of Single Adults

After serving at Knox Presbyterian Church in Los Angeles for ten years, I knew it was time for a change. I had served as a youth director part-time for two years while in seminary, as Assistant Pastor, Associate Pastor and my final 1 ½ years as the Interim Pastor. I decided to apply for the Air Force Chaplaincy, and though accepted, there were no active duty slots for the Presbyterian Church. I told the Presbyterian Chaplain board I would serve in the Reserves until a slot opened up. They said it would be at least 3-4 years. I put together my ministerial dossier and blitzed it out all over the United States. Although I did not apply for the Minister of Single Adults in Colorado Springs because they wanted someone with experience in a church of 1,000 or bigger, my dossier matched their skill list.

I was in my office at Knox Pres when the phone rang and John Stevens, Senior minister from First Pres in Colorado Springs, called to discuss the job with me. After a 30-minute conversation, he wanted the search committee to talk with me. I went home for lunch and mentioned to Marsha that First Pres in Colorado Springs had called. She said, "You did not apply for that job." I had applied for the job in Boulder, Colorado, but not this job. The search committee narrowed down the applicants from 300 to 3 and I was still in the running. Marsha and I ended up flying out to First Pres for an in-depth interview over a weekend and John Stevens picked us up at the airport and took us to his house that night for dinner. I ended up teaching the Going Concern class on Sunday, 300-350 singles, on the Lord's Prayer. After all these interviews and travel, God chose me to be their new Minister of Single Adults.

This was truly a God thing, as I had no experience in Singles Ministry.

When I started this new ministry in August 1981, there were approximately 1000 singles I was responsible for. There was the Growing Edge, ages 25-40 and mostly never married, with 300 singles; The Going Concern, ages 35-60 and mainly divorced singles, with 600 singles; and the Widows and widowers, 100 who belonged to a monthly activity group. To supply the Going Concern class, two Divorce Recovery Workshops (DRW) were offered twice a year to the community. In the early 1980s, single ministry was just getting started in the United States and First Pres had one of the largest. The DRW would draw an average of 300 divorce people into the 7-week session. I remember the first time I spoke at the DRW, I recall there was more pain per square inch in that room than any other time I spoke. Most people were hurting and did not want to be there but knew they must. By session #7, the topic was forgiveness, and there was warm laughter in the room that was absent before. This was the hardest topic to hear but necessary for healing. Our goal for the DRW was we wanted people to not just go through divorce but grow through divorce.

We were the only church in town that had a Single's Ministry, so we were often labeled as the "meat market" in town. It's amazing how evil wants to attack and destroy a good ministry. Even the elders and leadership of First Pres were threatened by the Single's Ministry, afraid it might take over the church. Those were challenging times as God was blessing the ministry and as a result, we were being attacked.

I was blessed with a wonderful young lady, Marilyn Levan, to assist me in this huge ministry. She was very talented with a beautiful voice and led music at our numerous retreats during the four years I was there. She also had a heart and schooling for counseling and we both did more than our share of counseling for these singles who were emotionally bleeding. Besides the biannual retreats at Trail West we had for each of the single's groups, there were also mission trips we sponsored. Some of these trips were in-state for a weekend mission project, plus we had yearly week-long mission trips to out-of-state places. These mission trips were critical in helping singles grow deeper in their faith and commitment to God.

Besides the many retreats and mission trips that occurred, singles have lots of free time and a need for fellowship with others. This meant we planned numerous social events which packed our calendars. Every weekend and many nights were filled with activities. My schedule was overloaded, and I was working 75 to 80-hour weeks. But in spite of my incredibly busy schedule I made sure my family was first on my focus. This was very challenging at times, but I ensured when the girls were having a show at school to be present and supportive. In addition to my singles ministries, I was also responsible for assisting in leading worship each Sunday, attending the Sunday evening services, and teaching on Wednesday nights a subject of my choice.

My Single Ministry went from overseeing 1000 to being responsible for 1400 singles before I left First Pres in July 1985. We not only had a DRW for adults but also created a support ministry for children and youth as their parents went through this difficult time. The children and youth had a support system at the same time as their parents. This was critical for young people to stay strong during this time and not blame themselves for the divorce. We also created a "Going through Grief" workshop designed with the same format as the DRW having a lecture followed by small groups with two facilitators where the real healing happened. God was blessing this single's ministry during the early 1980s. The Spirit was bringing not only healing from divorce and grief but many of these singles became Christians too. This was a powerful ministry. Unfortunately, it ultimately took its toll on my body and the neck of my bladder constricted and I had to have surgery in June 1985. My body had hit the wall after four years and I spent a week in the hospital to recover and mend. This was a very painful time in my life to watch my healthy body fall apart. I thought God would protect me from any danger if I was doing God's work. I was wrong and spent a week in the hospital from burnout. As a Type A person, I learned the hard way what happens when one violates the Sabbath. The Single Ministry was very exciting and fulfilling but it did cost me my physical wellbeing.

Air Force Flight in the Pacific

One of the things I loved the most as a chaplain in the Air Force was being able to fly as an essential personnel with the C-141 cargo plane called the "Starlifter." I was one of six personnel who flew out to the Pacific Ocean on a mission to move cargo from Norton Air Force Base in San Bernardino, California, to several islands. The trip originated at Norton AFB and flew to Hawaii, Guam, Japan and home again. It was normally a two-week trip as frequently an airplane would break down in the circuit, delaying all the planes behind it.

I was a young Captain in my 30s when I was invited to go on this trip. There was a pilot, co-pilot, and navigator up in the cockpit. In the back of the plane where all the cargo was carried, two crew chiefs were responsible for loading and off-loading the cargo. When in the back of the plane with the cargo, you wore earplugs because of the jet noise and sat in web seats alongside the airplane.

Before each flight, there was always a briefing that the pilot would inform the crew of the purpose of the mission and any special directions. On this flight, the pilot was a Major and said to me during the briefing, "Chaplain, I am not thrilled that you are on this mission with us. Just stay out of my way." I thought, wow, thanks a lot for a cold welcome. I discovered later on during the flight that he was a chain smoker in the cockpit, so I chose not to stay up there very long. Unfortunately, whenever we landed at our new base, he bought a six pack of beer and went to his room and drank it. I hung around with the co-pilot and other team members and found out that Bob had just gone through a divorce and was very angry and unhappy. This was a sad way to live. During the flights, I decided that I was going to pray for Bob and his dilemma and befriend him. A couple of times, we got up at 4am for a 6 am take off only to discover that the flight had been cancelled, so we ate breakfast together and made the best of the day ahead. This ended up being a great opportunity to get to know the guys, including Bob.

As the trip went on, Bob started to warm up to me as a chaplain. In fact, we were supposed to be back at Norton AFB but because of two delays, I would not be able to preach this coming Sunday. Bob called my boss and asked for special permission for me to stay with his crew because, as he said, "Chaplain Markwalder is too valuable a person to loose on this mission." I was shocked as this was the same person who 12 days earlier was not for me being part of his crew. God showed up and did great work in Bob's life. Praise the Lord!!

Hawaiian Family Trip

One year after I went on active duty to Norton Air Force Base in San Bernardino, California, we made plans to fly to Hawaii as a family. One of the big perks of being on active duty in the Air Force was the cheaper lodging and plane travel you get. So, we booked lodging at Billows Air Force Base (AFB) in Hawaii and signed up for Space-A travel. Billows AFB was a small place with lodging for military members, active, reserve, and retired. The individual cottages were located right along the sandy beach and they would sleep six people. At night, you could hear the breaking of the waves and the wind which blew open your curtains. The floors were tile because you would track sand in from outside. They were nothing fancy, but the price was right. Back in 1986, when we went, it was only $50 a night for the whole family. They included a small kitchen and there was a grocery store within walking distance, so we ate most meals at the cozy cottage.

Getting over to Hawaii was a different challenge. We drove our motor home up to Travis AFB close to San Francisco, which offered the best chance of getting on an Air Force plane for only $10 a person. Unfortunately, when we went in the summer, our children were out of school, but so were hundreds of other kids. When we signed up for the flight at Travis AFB, we were a whopping 1900 on the list. They said a list that long usually takes about four days for your number to come up. So we drove to San Jose, California, which was only 80 miles away and visited our parents. After four days, we returned only to discover they were now helping the 1200s. This was very disappointing, so we looked for other options since we still had our lodging on hold at Billows AFB. Someone told us to go to San Francisco airport and fly to

Hawaii in a standby status for the military. We thought, let's give that a try, as we still wanted to go. Fortunately, we found a commercial airline that had five seats in standby status for $150 each, so we took it. This was a lot more than $10 each but way cheaper than $400 a person, which was the regular cost.

We got aboard and made it to Hawaii for the first time for our children. When we got off the plane in Hawaii, it was so warm and humid that someone said it felt like we went into a sauna. We enjoyed our stay at Billows and bonded as a family. We loved playing in the waves together and trying to body surf in the warm water. We were told that jellyfish had been spotted in our area but that did not slow us down. I went and rented three boogie boards to ride the waves that were mild. Unfortunately, when I returned with the boards, all three of our girls had just been stung by jellyfish and were no longer interested in staying in the refreshing waters.

Normally, we ate dinner at the cottage, but on one occasion, we ate at the nearby officers club. The food was delicious and the entertainment was superb: karaoke from volunteers who were eating there. Guess who we were blessed to hear sing? Yes, Dave's angels gave it a whirl and were good with all the actions included.

After being in Hawaii for a week, it was time to say "Aloha" and leave Hawaii. This time, we signed up two days beforehand and our number to fly on an Air Force plane for $10 each came up. The only challenge was the rental car we rented came from the commercial airport which was ten miles away from Hickam AFB airport. So I got the family all checked in at the terminal and then returned the rental car ten miles away. The only glitch was I needed to catch a ride back to Hickam AFB.

After speaking to some people at a nearby hamburger stand and offering to pay them to take me over to Hickam AFB, I finally found a person who agreed that I would sit in the back of his pick-up truck as there was no room in the cab. Here I was in my blue Air Force uniform, riding down the freeway in the back of a truck, holding on to my hat. What was really hysterical is when we got to the security gate at Hickam AFB, the security police saluted me and waved us through as he shook his head. That was probably the first time he had ever seen an officer riding in the back of a pickup truck. When we got to the airport, I jumped out of the truck, handed the man the money and ran to my family in the terminal just in time to make the plane. They were sweating it too, as they could not board the plane without me. We barely made it but for a total fee of only $50, it was well worth it to get us home. That was our first experience flying Space-A with the Air Force. This benefit is excellent if you are retired and do not have any schedule to meet. It is also good for personnel with no children and can fly during the off-season when it is not busy. But I'm glad we did it and we did enjoy Honolulu and staying at Billows AFB.

South Korea Trip

I had served as a Reserve Air Force chaplain for four years while serving the First Presbyterian Church in Colorado Springs. I served one day a month at Peterson Air Force Base (AFB), mainly visiting the troops at their job. This was called "Ministry of Presence" and allowed us to talk with military personnel while working, sometimes leading to an on-the-spot counseling situation. I also did two weeks in the summer at Peterson AFB. I preached in the chapel, did counseling and did lots of visitation, which was my favorite part of my job. It was a joy to rub shoulders with many new people and often have the privilege of helping them out.

After four years as a Reserve Chaplain, I was called up to go on active duty as a Captain in the Air Force. My first assignment was at Norton AFB in San Bernardino, California. My wife and I met many new friends at this active base to support the flying mission of C141 cargo planes. The base aimed to fly cargo to numerous islands in the Pacific Ocean like Hawaii, Guam, Okinawa, and Japan.

One of our neighbor's on-base housing was the Vincent's. I thought it quite appropriate that we lived on Samaritan Court. The main drawback of this assignment was the heavy smog that covered us in the spring and summer. It was so bad that your eyes would burn and your chess would hurt if you exercised outside in the swimming pool. The mountains behind us were often invisible because of the smog. It reminded me of my graduate study days in Pasadena in the early 1970's.

The Air Force is notorious for moving personnel often and our new neighbors, the Vincents, had orders to move to South

Korea. The Air Force is one big happy family and people you meet often invite them to visit them at their new location. This was true of the Vincents, who told us to come and see them anytime. So we took them up on their invitation and planned a trip to South Korea.

In 1987, our three daughters were 11, 9 and 9. We were blessed when one of the twin's teachers, Mrs. Williams, offered to take care of the girls during spring break while we were gone. It was close to Easter time when we left and we remember celebrating a Passover meal with our Catholic friends at the chapel in Soul Korea. Talk about a neat experience that crossed all religious barriers.

In order to get to South Korea, we flew "Space-A" (Available) on a C141 cargo plane with 30 Marines and their equipment. This was definitely the cheapest way to fly, only $10 each, but you had to wear earplugs because of the noisy aircraft and sit on red web seats along both sides. The price was right but it lacked comfort and took two days to reach our destination after stopping at Hickam AFB in Hawaii and Midway Island. But this was one experience that I would not trade.

Once we got to South Korea, we had a nice visit with our friends. Besides the unique experience of a Seder dinner at the chapel, the other outstanding adventure was the shopping. We bought numerous puppets for $3-4 that we shipped to our missionaries in Mexico for their children's ministry. They were thrilled to receive this valuable package that helped make an impact on many children. Besides the incredibly cheap puppets, the normal price in US was $20 each; we bought three large white bears for only $6 each, which was $30 in the States. We visited South Korea 1 ½ years before the summer Olympics. After that event, the prices increased on many of their items.

Marsha and I also found some incredible deals on dresses for her in the downtown area of Soul, Korea. We bought several sweater suits for $20 each, which would have cost us at least $80 in America. One of the reasons they were so reasonable was that most Korean women are short and these dresses were for tall women, which was perfect for Marsha. The sales ladies were very excited to see us when we went in these shops. I had to tell Marsha to leave so I could barter with the women without her presence. It was harder for Marsha to negotiate prices than for me. I rather enjoyed the experience of getting good deals.

Our trip home was much easier as we boarded a 747 contract plane that got us home in 15 hours of flying. It was good to get back home and be with our girls again. They loved all our gifts to them, including the three big bears.

Marco Polo at Norton AFB

It was the summer of 1988, and we were getting ready to leave Norton AFB in San Bernardino, CA. But before leaving, we needed one more swim in the pool that we spent hours enjoying in the hot sun. Unfortunately, there was also much smog that affected our lungs and eyes. We enjoyed playing "Marco Polo" in the pool's shallow end. Our whole family got involved in this game and no one was left out. This game was fun for everyone and the pool felt great in the day's heat.

I remember calling out "Marco" and waited to hear the response "Polo," so I would know which way to swim to catch my next victim. The girls were very good swimmers and many times, would go under the water to avoid being caught. They also were skilled at working as a team to trick the person calling out. We spent hours in that pool playing this game and enjoying the refreshing water. They were very quiet and clever at avoiding being caught. Sometimes, I would have to fake going in one direction to see if I could hear any splashing and giggles as they were determined to avoid being captured.

After several minutes would go by, I would peek out of one eye just to make sure they were still in the pool. They were and were difficult to tag. I was finally relieved when I caught someone and was no longer it. This was a fun game that we all enjoyed playing.

Homer, Alaska Trip 1988

One of the benefits of serving in the Air Force on active duty is access to Space Available on cargo airplanes for my family and me. During the summer of 1988, we planned a vacation to Homer, Alaska, to visit one of our former neighbors in Los Angeles. Lorraine Weber lived on the same street when I was a pastor at Knox Presbyterian Church and she had two girls the same age as our daughters. Since Lorraine had a full-time educator job, Marsha often took care of her girls after school. The five girls enjoyed playing with each other at our home. This was before we moved to Colorado in 1981.

We had always wanted to visit Alaska and now was our chance to fly aboard a large cargo plane from Travis Air Force Base by San Francisco to Anchorage, Alaska, for $10 each. The seats were sitting backwards but it was more comfortable than sitting on the web seats on the side of the airplane. This aircraft was a C5 and the largest aircraft in the Air Force at the time. They installed approximately 60 passenger seats for the four-hour flight. Unfortunately, the airplane did experience quite a bit of turbulence and all my ladies got air sickness.

When we landed at Elmendorf Air Force base, I rented a car for our 5-hour drive from Anchorage to Homer. It was a very scenic drive as we traveled along the beautiful snowcapped mountains that reminded us of the Colorado Rockies. Once we got to Homer, it was a friendly reunion to see Lorraine and her two girls, Kim and Wendy. We also met Lorraine's new husband, who was a high school crony. He was a boat captain and would take people on tours of their scenic bay.

Homer, Alaska, is the capital of Halibut fish. One evening we were treated to a delicious fish feast of fresh Halibut cooked on the barbeque. It was incredibly delicious and some of the best-cooked fish we have ever eaten. It melted in your mouth and tasted oh-so-good. I also remember their house being at the end of a long dirt road that was uphill and perfect for running. I was currently in training to run the Pikes Peak Ascent in August when we returned from our trip to Homer. Unfortunately, Homer is at sea level and the Pike Peak Ascent race starts at 6500 feet and goes to 14,200 feet. Being on vacation to California and Alaska for two weeks before the race did not help my training.

I remember feeling out of breath in my first three miles in the race. This was going to be ugly and not a good sign. I discovered training at sea level two weeks before my first race was not smart. At least I finished the race, but the last three miles, called the Golden Stair Steps, were brutal. Then, I remembered the words from a good friend who had run this race numerous times, "Dave, remember the mountain will always win."

After saying goodbye to our good friends in Homer, we got in the car and drove back to Anchorage to wait at Elmendorf Air Force Base for our return flight. We signed up to wait our turn until an airplane had enough empty seats to allow us to board. The price for taking a Space Available Air Force plane is cheap, but you must be patient most of the time until the seats are available. This happened to us and we needed to spend overnight in the terminal until our airplane was ready for us the next day. You can only watch so many summer Olympics from Soul Korea in the airport terminal. We ended up having our girls sleep under the cribs in the Nursery area, which was the best available location for heat. This whole trip was another adventure for the Markwalder family to enjoy.

Racing up Pikes Peak

Each year in August, Colorado Springs hosts an annual race up Bar Trail to the top of Pikes Peak. My good friend Don Wallace said, "The Mountain will always win." This is a truth that one has to learn the hard way by running up the mountain. Actually, it is more of a fast walk up the trail that extends for 13.6 miles to the summit. There are a few times you can jog it slowly but for the most part, you are walking at a fast pace.

The race begins in Manitou Springs, which is 7000' and finishes at the top of Pikes Peak at a whopping 14,150' above sea level. On my journey up the hill I noticed the further I climbed, the harder my heart was beating. The air gets very rare the higher you go. Unfortunately, I made a grave mistake before the race and traveled to California and Alaska where the elevation is a lot lower than Colorado Springs. So, as I started the race, I felt I was clearly at a disadvantage, having been at sea level for several weeks.

I thought oh boy, this is going to be a tough race up this hill. But I had committed myself to run it so here I go. How am I going to survive this if I am already feeling the altitude? But I had worked too hard to stop now, so I continued the race one grueling step at a time. By the time I had reached the trail head for the race, I was winded, moving slowly but steadily. I looked around and found someone to keep up with at a steady gate. Then I got my second wind as we passed the Cog Rail Station, where people had arrived to travel up the peak by the train. I thought how lucky these people are to ride to the top and enjoy the view.

The first half of the race was hard but nothing compared to what was ahead. It is a good thing I did not know what was coming or I probably would have turned around and walked to the bottom of the trail. But onward and upward, I went going through a beautiful meadow of trees and shrubs. This was definitely my favorite part of the trip. Not only was there nice scenery to run through but the trail had leveled off some, which felt good. It gave me hope that I could finish this insane race. Pat yourself on the back, Dave. You are actually doing this incredibly difficult race.

It was 13.6 miles up the mountain and climbed an impressive 7,000 feet. When you arrive at BAR Camp, you are half way to the top. It is time for a brief stop and enjoy some refreshments of power bars or whatever you can eat putting important calories and energy in your burning machine. Some people even laid down for a brief rest but I chose to keep on chugging up the hill one foot at a time. I was afraid if I got down, I might not get back up, so onward I went, fighting the temptation to stop.

The next part of the race was much harder as the elevation was above 10,000 ft. As I continued up, up and up to the summit, I noticed there were quite a few people who had sat down on the side of the trail to catch their breath. I was tempted to join them but I knew if I did, it would be very difficult to start again. So I kept going up the hill and started to silently pray "The Lord's Prayer," Psalm 23, and other verses to keep my mind on something positive in the midst of my pain. I started to ask myself, "Why are you doing this?" It was the first time I ran this race and I did it three more times before I learned that I don't need to put myself through physical torture.

Who was I trying to impress? Why put myself through so much pain and torture? Next came the "The 14 Golden Stairsteps," which is a totally misleading title. This happens right before you get to the summit and challenges you with numerous big boulders you need to climb over. I thought to myself, "Whoever came up with that title was delirious from the high altitude. Glad that was behind me as I moved on to the top and finished this race. They say that doing this race is equivalent to running a 26.2 marathon race.

A very nice surprise awaited all of us who made it to the top of Pikes Peak, America's Mountain. Not only was there a spectacular view of the land below but one could see how Kate Smith got her inspiration to write "America, America." This is one of the truly great national anthems that shares the beauty of the United States. In addition, there were good refreshments awaiting all of us who climbed this challenging hill. Everything from fresh orange slices, water melon, water, Gatorade, M&M's. and protein bars were awaiting us to help us regain our energy which was depleted.

A Shocking Surprise

On September 11, 1988, my father, Edwin Markwalder, died from a massive heart attack. The reason it was so shocking is that Dad had only been in the hospital once when he had prostate problems. Other than that, he was perfectly healthy. His blood pressure was a bit high but I thought it was because he salted everything. As a plant accountant for Continental Can Company (CCC), his stress level seemed to be normal. He worked for CCC for 35 years before retiring. Dad enjoyed doing yard work, which was his main exercise. He also helped his parents with their six lots of property, producing numerous trees and vegetables. He loved to take our family camping for two weeks at Tuolumne Meadows above Yosemite National Park for pure relaxation. We would go with another family and Dad went fishing every day up in the high Sierra Mountains. This was very satisfying to Dad and helped him unwind and relax.

They would often drive to the trailhead, walk 3-4 miles to a pristine lake, and be the only two fishermen there. The fresh air from the pine trees was invigorating during the hike. Even getting only a few bites when fishing would make it a good day. It was God's beautiful creation that brought Dad great contentment. He was a very patient man and enjoyed the solitude and serene setting.

When I got the phone call that dad had a massive heart attack and was dying, I was totally shocked. He was 77 years old, had been retired for 15 years, and enjoyed life with his wife, Edna, of 45 years. He had worked hard and was finally getting to enjoy the reward of having time to do things of his choosing. They started to travel more and spend more time with relatives and friends. At first, I could not believe the news as Dad was feeling well and enjoying life. There were no symptoms of heart disease that he was worried about. But on a hot afternoon, he took his van to pick up some fertilizer for his yard. After getting several bags on his cart, he went to deliver them to his van. Although there was a young lady to assist him in carrying the heavy bags to the van, Dad was such a gentleman and insisted on doing it himself. Unfortunately, between the heat and his blood pressure being elevated, it caused a massive heart attack. There was an off-duty sheriff who gave him CPR but the attack was too severe and Dad died shortly afterwards at the hospital.

I felt so sorry for my mother, who was grieving deeply in losing Dad. Unfortunately, she was overly dependent on Dad for finances, driving and many other areas of their lives. Mother was 72 and became depressed and deeply affected by Dad's death. After the funeral in San Jose, CA, in which I gave the eulogy, Harold shared a message on Psalm 23 and Marsha played the Lord's Prayer on her violin, I stayed with Mother for two weeks. During this time, I tried to help with her finances, did lots of plumbing work on leaky faucets and toilets, and gave her moral and emotional support with my older sister Carol. These were challenging days but we kept busy and did what we could to bring stability in a chaotic time.

My father was a very good violinist so it was very fitting that Marsha played her violin at the funeral. The mortuary was packed with over 300 people who came to say their goodbyes to Dad and support Mom. Because Dad had parents with good genes, Grandpa Markwalder died at age 86 and Grandma Markwalder died at age 93, we thought Dad would live to be 90 or older. This is a reminder to be grateful for each day you have to live and not to take life and health for granted. My father was a good man with a strong faith who loved and supported his family.

Two Extreme Remote Assignments

In 1989, I had the privilege of going to two opposite parts of the world as an Air Force chaplain. I was currently a Reserve Chaplain and I was not a pastor of any church, which meant I was free to accept any assignments to support our military personnel. Two openings happened within six months of each other. The first one, I had orders to go to Thule, Greenland, over Lent and Easter. My second order had me going to South

West Asia in late summer. I was gone from my family for 175 days that year.

After getting special training and proper dress and equipment, I was on my way to Greenland for two months to help cover the Easter season for military personnel and numerous civilian contractors from Denmark. Greenland is covered with sheets of ice and snow. One learns to dress warm and safe in the frigid weather. There were extreme temperatures of 70 degrees below with a wind chill. When it was this cold, the warning went out to wear proper dress or you could die if outdoors within 3-4 minutes. When dressed appropriately in this brutally cold weather, it is amazing how warm you can be with mucalet boots, gloves, heavy coats, and an excellent hoody with a fir lining. The temperature was so cold that all vehicles needed to be plugged into an electrical outlet when not driving.

One of the amazing surprises of that area is how clear the air is. You could see large glaciers that looked only two miles away but in reality, the distance was 20 miles. The air was extremely dry, which led us to drink lots of water to keep hydrated. The mission of Thule was to be a constant watchguard for any Russian aircraft. There were large, isolated radar installations built on the ice. Personnel would be assigned out there for six months to a year at a time. When we visited one of the sites to bring supplies to them with a C130 ski plane, they were excited to see us. Loneliness plagued individuals, and talking and encouraging them in their mission was important.

At the end of the summer, it was time to be "on the road again," but this time to South West Asia, where the temperatures were just the opposite of Thule, Greenland. I was sent to a remote site out in the middle of the Egyptian desert as the only chaplain for 120 Air Force personnel. The purpose of this base was to stock up on supplies in case of a war in a nearby region. Unlike Thule, the temperature ranged from 120 – 144 degrees. Most of the rooms for dinning and offices were underground because of the extreme heat. As the only chaplain, I provided worship services for Protestants, Catholics and Jews.

My mode of transportation was a bicycle, which I was glad to have. This was much better than trying to walk the six miles to visit personnel at their work sites. One of the challenges was there were scorpions and a two-step snake that kept you vigilant. They said if you were bitten by one of these snakes, you only had two steps to take before death. To say the least, one was very careful where you walked. The greatest problem the military personnel were challenged with was depression from loneliness. It was a one-year assignment for these good people and they longed to be home in better surroundings. But they served with valor for their country to provide freedom for its citizens.

CHAPEL
T-010

Travels in the Motorhome

We bought a used 1977, 20' motorhome in 1984 and planned to use it for camping with the family. We bought it from a private party and it seemed very clean and well cared for the number of miles it had on it. I discovered later on the odometer had already been around once. So, instead of having 46,000, it actually had 146,000. But it was ideal for our young family, driving from Colorado to California for Christmas and summer vacations.

It was a fun vehicle to take care of and use for family outings. One of our first trips in it was a 7,500 mile trip to see Mount Rushmore, across Canada to see the incredible Niagara Falls, then up to Boston to visit the Bussells. We started rocky when one of our dual rear tires blew out on the freeway. Fortunately, the next off-ramp had a tire store, so we were able to get it replaced without spending much time or money. It had tires on sale so we quickly replaced it. This was just one way

God was watching over us on this trip. It felt good to have a brand-new tire on the rear.

Our next stop was Mount Rushmore to visit the incredible carvings of four presidents: George Washington, Thomas Jefferson, Abraham Lincoln, and Theodore Roosevelt. Seeing those 60' carvings in the mountain was breathtaking. It was an awesome sight and I'm glad we took our girls on this trip. History and geography combined to make this a good trip. After watching the incredible sights of Mount Rushmore, it was time to get back in our orange carriage and travel to Rochester, Minnesota, where my mother was raised.

When we arrived there, we were greeted by several relatives who were glad to see us and welcomed us into their homes. We spent several days there enjoying fresh baked rolls for breakfast that Uncle Francis had mastered over his lifetime in the bakery business. What a great way to start the day. We enjoyed meeting the relatives and visiting their homes. We discovered that Rochester is a small town USA with the Mayo Clinic as its pride. We enjoyed our time meeting the relatives and visiting Uncle Lyndon's farm with all the animals. We picked my mother up as she had been visiting her brother Harold Washburn and younger brother Francis.

We got back in the Motorhome and continued our journey north to Niagara Falls to witness one of the wonders of the world. Hard to believe thousands of gallons of water going over the edge and crashing down hundreds of feet below every minute. To add to the excitement, a daredevil walked across on a tight rope hundreds of feet above it. Fortunately, he made it across without any incident, just thousands of nervous watchers. After watching the incredible sights of Niagara Falls, it was time to get back in our orange carriage and travel to Boston, Massachusetts, to visit the Bussell family.

Second Day in the Motorhome

We enjoyed seeing many sights and sounds, like walking on the Freedom Trail and enjoying fresh lobster sandwiches in their mall downtown. YUM!! Then, another day, we went to a quaint fish and chip place in a small nearby town. My sister Carol cooked up a fabulous scallop dish for dinner the next day. We were treated like royal guests. We also went to a nearby beach and watched our kids and their cousins, Monique and Bradford, play in the ocean. What fun to hear them laugh and scream as the water got them wet. After enjoying our time with them, we said our goodbyes and continued on our trip south to New York City.

When we arrived in New York City, we were greeted by a very congested freeway that was stop-and-go for two long hours. The girls were totally aghast at watching people get out of their cars and run to the bushes on the side of the road to go to the bathroom. This was a real shocker. The next day, we met up with the Walberg family who we lived next door to at Norton Air Force Base. They were now stationed at McGuire Air Force Base in New Jersey so they toured the Statue of Liberty with us. It was great to see them again after several years. The Statue of Liberty was very large and impressive, representing America's freedom. After being in New York City for a few days, it was time to continue south to Washington, DC.

We arrived at the capitol on July 4th just in time to take in all the Independence celebration. The day we arrived was overcast and gloomy. We were hoping that the weather would clear up so the planned fireworks would happen. Fortunately, that happened but in the meantime, there was lots of rain on the Washington mall and nothing to hide under, only soggy grass to walk on and get our feet wet. But the rain was warm so we were okay. The worst part of it was when we were crossing a bridge and a car came by and splashed us, which got us entirely soaked. But it was warm and we were already wet, so little harm was done.

We did lots of walking that day and visited the many unique areas of the mall. The one that was the biggest hit was the air museum, which has numerous old artifacts from a mockup of the Wright brother's airplane, the Kitty Hawk, and several others. This was a mega history museum of airpower and the development of the airplane. We learned a lot that day about planes and their importance for human transportation.

When it got dark, it was time to get ready for the fireworks. The program was overwhelming, with many fireworks of grand finales. What a great way to end the 4th of July in Washington, DC. No one was disappointed but thrilled by a great display. Then, it was time to get in the motorhome and get some shut-eye before another big day of travel.

After all the walking we did on July 4th, it was good to have a day of travel. So, after breakfast we got on the road and headed for Virginia to visit our Knox Presbyterian Church friends, the Pingels. Rich and Jan were a large part of our Knox Church young married class. They had two children, Thad, who was the youngest and Anna. They invited us to go swimming with them in their pool. After swimming and getting some sun, it was time for dinner. They served "Spaghetti Pie." What was really cute was how Thad said haven't you ever had "Spaghetti Pie" before with his Virginia accent. It made all of us laugh and ask what?

The next morning, after breakfast, we thanked them for the visit and said our good byes. Then we got in the orange pumpkin and got on the road again. This time, we were headed for an RV park to play games and stay overnight. Before night time, I'll never forget putting the girls in their boats and pushing them out in the water. The only problem is somehow Star got split between the dock and the boat. Soon, she was doing the spits and landed in the water. To say the least, she was not a happy camper. Oh well. Just another funny memory for a great five weeks of fun on the road with the family.

Then there was the time when Jewel was sitting in the front with me and the fire extinguisher went off and sprayed Jewel. It was a riveting moment, for sure. These were just two funny clips of our motorhome experience. Good memories to bond us as a family.

After traveling 7,500 miles and three weeks, we were thrilled to be home with minimum mishaps. I think it is time to go on another motorhome trip. What say you girls?

From Rags to Riches

In 1990, Marsha and I were at the bottom of the cellar financially. Marsha was working at Markwalder's Artistic Creation which was a ceramic business creating all kinds of ceramics to sell at Blue Columbine in Colorado City, Platte Floral, Flowers to Go, and a shop at Estes Park. We sold $28,000 in one year, plus we did a Christmas show at the Denver Convention Center and sold $5,000 over a 3-day weekend. We used our Dodge Broham Motorhome to load up all the ceramics and two heavy 6' tables to display the merchandise on. Ceramics were a lot of work setting up and taking down because they were very fragile. Especially, when we did week-end shows like Territory Days in Colorado City that were outside. The wind was not our friend as the ceramics were very breakable when they got knocked off the table.

We had two large Kilns that were located in the basement of our home at 538 Silver Spring Circle to heat up our ceramic products. During the cold months, the Kilns helped to heat our home. Although Marsha created some very beautiful ceramic pieces, it was labor-intensive. She would create products for all the different seasons, like Christmas (Angels), Easter (Rabbits), Halloween (Jack-o-lanterns), Thanksgiving (Pumpkin Candles & Turkeys) and Mother's Day (Violet Pots). In addition, she created large ducks, flower pots and much more. I helped with the pouring of the slip into the molds and emptying them after sitting for several hours. Some of the larger molds were hernia makers weighing 50-60 lbs. The slip itself came in 5-gallon buckets and was extremely heavy. The only reason we were able to sell $28,000 in our best year was because we kept the overhead to a minimum by owning our own kilns, pouring tables and tools to make the ceramics.

We worked extremely hard and put in 70 to 80 hours weekly to make the business successful. From 1988-1990, I was also gone a lot with the Air Force mission. One year, I was gone for 150 days and the next year, it was 175 days. As a chaplain, I was open to serving our country in any way I could. In the same year, I went to Thule and Soderstrum, Greenland, over Easter for two months, where the weather got down to a minus 70 wind chill factor out on the ice-covered continent. The warning was to dress appropriately or you could die within four minutes.

After returning home, I also did construction on fixing up a large home near Cheyenne Mountain High School. Gary Bader found the job for me and I was paid $15/hour. I did painting the outside of the home, refinished and stained a large deck overlooking the forest, brick work and whatever needed to be done. This helped put groceries on the table. I also helped Marsha with the ceramic business. After a few months, it was time to leave again only this time to a desert in Egypt where I was the only chaplain for 120 Air Force soldiers in this remote site close to the Red Sea. I was given a bicycle to get around and visit the troops on this Old Russian base. In contrast to Greenland, the temperature was always over 100 degrees and one day it reached 144 degrees. Once it gets over 120 degrees, you can't tell the difference. All the rooms, like the dining room, were underground for the coolness. I volunteered to help serve the meals as the soldiers would come by to get their food. This helped me to get a high visibility in seeing all the troops for dinner. I did both the Protestant and Catholic services on Friday, which was the holy day in Egypt. These soldiers were here for a one-year remote tour as they could not bring their families. As a result, the greatest thing they struggled with was depression. That is a long time being away from your family whom you love. I did a lot of counseling with the troops.

I had a trailer I slept in and an adjoining room for the worship services. There were scorpions, so you had to make sure you shook out your boots before putting them on. There was also a two-step snake and if you accidently stepped on it you had only two steps before dying. So you were very cautious wherever you walked.

These were two hard years for Marsha and me but we survived. Unfortunately, our income was very low and we literally had money to put food on the table after paying our bills. Our girls experienced the value of a dollar. We did the best we could but at times, it was pretty bleak. Since I did not have a full-time job at a church, the general at the 302nd Tactical Wing that I served part-time said, "Dave, I want to send you to Air Command and Staff College in Montgomery, Alabama, for ten months." It is a training school for 800 majors in the Air Force to help them fulfill their education for promotion to Lt. Col. This was a full-time job and I would get full-time pay, which was like a gold mine. The opportunity was too good to pass up and the government would move my family there if they wanted to go. I asked our three daughters if they wanted to go with me and they quickly responded, "Dad, we love you, but we are going to miss you."

Beginning in August of 1990, I drove our 20' motor home and pulled the VW bug behind it to Air University to set up my home at the Family Camp for the next ten months. The government would only pay for one housing allowance and this was the cheapest way for me to live for only $150/month. I had all the comforts of home, except it was very hot and humid there for the first two months. I did not have any A/C but only a large fan to try and keep the motorhome comfortable. I remember my initiation to camping in Alabama happened when I felt what I thought was a mosquito that bit my neck in the middle of the night. Unfortunately, it was a fire ant that bit me so I quickly striped off my sheet to discover a trail of fire ants on my feet. They had climbed up the front wheel well and were attacking me. I had to spray the whole area at 1 am before going back to bed. This was not a fun but a memorable experience.

Although this was a difficult time for our family, we made the best of it. I had the family fly out to see me for Christmas and we drove to Disney World in Florida. This was a great trip for all of us. I had not seen the family since Thanksgiving when I flew home. Having a full-time job with the Air Force and Marsha working with Markwalder's Artistic Creation helped us slowly get out of our financial hole.

As a result of me being willing to go to Air Command and Staff College in residence, God opened up the door for my next assignment in the Air Force, which was in Denver, CO, at Lowry AFB. This was a 70-mile commute and I drove this route for 12 years to Air Reserve Personnel Command. This allowed the girls to attend Eagle View Middle School and Air Academy High School with their friends. They also enjoyed being close to their church friends at First Presbyterian Church in Colorado Springs. I was blessed with this Air Force job that was only guaranteed for four years at a time, but I was extended on the job twice for 12 years. The down side is I had to leave home by 5:30 am to get to my job by 7:30. There were times when it snowed and the commute ended up 2 ½ hours each way. Fortunately, I had several different car pool cohorts who commuted from Colorado Springs too. My first buddy was Bill Hume who was a lawyer and lived in Glen Eagle. Then I had Ann Shippy and Mike Gebhardt. There were other folks who were with us for a shorter term. But God was faithful and I was blessed with many people who shared the challenge of community together.

After having Markwalder's Artistic Creations for five years, the real estate market finally turned around and became positive again. I told Marsha, "You have always wanted to be a realtor, so why don't you go to real estate school and get your license? A buck an hour in our ceramic business is not going to get our girls through college." I was proud of Marsha as she stepped out of her comfort zone, took the class, studied hard, and passed the exam to get her license. She had studied so hard that she went on and took the Broker test and passed it too.

The first couple years in real estate she worked for Heritage and made a few sales but nothing substantial. After three years, she switched to the big leagues and joined ReMax. From this change, her income mushroomed and eventually, she was making over $100,000 a year. Combine this with my Air Force income and we were making a fabulous income. We essentially lived off my income and invested her income for our future retirement. We chose not to increase our standard of living, which was a really good decision. I thoroughly enjoyed my job in the Air Force as the head recruiter for Chaplain Candidates in seminary and Reserve Chaplains. I had the best job as I got to fly to various Christian colleges and seminaries in the United States, which minimized my commuting. I had the privilege of shaping the future of the Air Force Chaplaincy.

As a result of Marsha's good salary and my Air Force income, we now have a fabulous retirement income. We have the privilege of generously supporting nine missionaries, three churches, three Compassion International children in Africa and Mexico, Westside Care ministries for the homeless, and three Christian Conference grounds. We can also afford to take trips on our bucket lists and visit incredible places in this beautiful world. This also allows us to support our family with generous gifts. We have discovered that you cannot out-give God. I believe one of the reasons we have been blessed is because we were faithful in tithing our income right from the start of our marriage. No matter how tight our finances were, we always put God first. He has been so good to Marsha and me down through the years.

Sponsored Air Force Cadets

From 1990-2003, we sponsored 25-26 cadets attending the Air Force Academy in Colorado Springs. We normally would sponsor two cadets a year for their four years when they attended the Air Force Academy. This program allows the cadets to get off campus and stay with the family that is sponsoring them, usually for a weekend. Since the cadets could not be married until after they graduated, and they could not have their own car until the beginning of their junior year, it was up to us to go and pick them up and drop them off for the weekend. Sponsoring a cadet was a big commitment of your time and your energy. We were still in our early 40s when we started this program, and we had plenty of energy to help the cadets. Sponsoring a cadet meant we became their family part-time to support them through these challenging times.

Our first two cadets were Paul Perkins and Julian Cheater, beginning in June of 1990. They were both from California, so we had something in common with them. Paul had been through three years of college, so was older and Julian was right out of high school. Paul was a real free spirit, and he had a hard time being yelled at by younger cadets and all the rules and regulations. Julian would come to our home and call Marsha "Mam" and me "Sir" although we told him to relax and call us Dave and Marsha. Paul would have half his uniform off by the time he was at our front door. He would also go to movies in his civilian clothes, which was a no-no until he was recognized in March of his freshmen year.

Paul also told me that he was an atheist because six months earlier, his mother had been killed in an automobile accident. Julian was raised a Catholic but did not have a personal commitment to Christ. I can't imagine going through the Air Force Academy with the last name Cheater, but he succeeded and became an F16 pilot in his career. What's really amazing is that Julian is now an Air Force Major General after serving for 28 years. YEA Julian. Paul stayed in the Air Force for 22 years and then retired as a Lt. Col. He went on to fly for Southwest Airlines for four years and then got a job to fly for Fed Ex to Asia. He and his family now live in Anchorage, Alaska, which was a dream come true.

On June 2, 2022, his daughter, Sarah, got married closed to San Jose, so Marsha and I flew out there for the wedding and then stayed to celebrate Marsha's dad's 95th birthday on June 5. When we were at the wedding, Paul shared some loving words about his daughter and new son-in-law at the reception. The last thing he shared from his cell phone were the words of love from 1 Corinthians 13. I turned to Marsha and said, "This is our atheist cadet." Paul is now on fire for Jesus. Here is a great example of loving someone into the kingdom.

Two Air Force Schools

There are three Professional Military Education (PME) courses that one needs to take if you are interested in being promoted. As a Captain, it is Squadron Officer School (SOS), which I did by correspondence. As a Major in the Air Force, I attended Air Command and Staff College (ACSC) at Air University in Montgomery, Alabama, in 1990 and stayed there for ten months. Since I did not have a church job and the general at Peterson Air Force Base recommended that I apply, I did so and was accepted. This meant I was away from my family from August 1990 to June 1991. I did get to come home on various holidays and had my family join me during Christmas to go to Disney World in Florida.

The separation was difficult but the education and meeting new people were very rewarding. During this year, I took various courses like leadership, Ethics, Air Power, Space Command, War fighting strategies, and numerous other subjects. It was like drinking from a fire hose as we constantly changed topics every month. Just when you were getting comfortable with one, it was time to take a test and move on to another subject. I was in this course with 800 other students from America and international officers from all over the world. As a chaplain, I was there foremost as a student, but I was also able to minister to fellow students who had lost a loved one or were faced with loneliness. I graduated with a PME degree and a civilian degree of a Master of Military Science.

Eleven years later, in 2002, I had the opportunity to attend Air University again as a Colonel and take Air War College (AWC). All three of my angels had left the home and Marsha was very busy in her real estate business, so I went by myself and shared quarters at a lady's home with Rich Gomez, a Navy officer who was also attending AWC. He was a commander, which is equivalent to a lieutenant colonel in the Air Force. He was a dedicated runner and ran 5-6 miles daily.

There were 300 of the finest Air Force officers along with a few Navy, Army and Marines, at the school. There were also 30-40 International Officers from all over the world. We were broken up into small seminars of twelve students and I sat between a student from Canada and a student from Saudi Arabia. This was a great opportunity to learn about other cultures as well as be a Christian witness among these sharp men and women. We were required to write a term paper and I wrote mine on "Total Force Chaplaincy." The theme of the paper was to integrate the active duty, reserves and National Guard chaplains in order to bring about a stronger chaplain core during the war time of Afghanistan. This helped the active duty chaplains from being spread too thin and gave the Reserve and Guard a great chance to gain valuable experience.

For my two-week country experience, I chose to go to China and learn about their Air Force and civilian leadership. Every student would choose to fly to a different country, learn about their culture, and share with them about our Air Force. This was an incredible experience as we got to meet with

China's Air Force leaders. I asked what freedom of religion looks like, which is mentioned in their constitution. After a long pause, he replied, "We are still in an infancy state in contrast to America." Basically, there is none and that is why most churches in China are underground.

Besides being in small group seminars for learning, we attended a large lecture hall to listen to top Air Force and civilian speakers. This was a very rich time of interesting speakers followed by question and answer time for 15-20 minutes. The floor was open and anyone was invited to ask questions on any subject, usually tying in with the discussed topic. There were a few of us who just couldn't help but stand up and ask our questions with a microphone. Most of my questions had to do with morality, integrity or faith and I was later thanked by fellow officers who wanted to ask the same question but were too afraid too. I ended up asking the most questions of my classmates.

Stranded in Dagget, CA

Jewel was driving the motorhome before we got to San Bernardino, CA, for Christmas when she said, "Dad, there is something wrong with the motorhome." I was lying in the back of the motorhome and told Jewel to slowly pull the vehicle over on the shoulder. It was 12:30 am and too dark to look for the problem. All night long, we would get pushed over by the wind when large trucks passed by us at 70 mph. This led to very little sleep. The next morning, a truck driver pulled over to try to help us. We discovered that most truck drivers were quite helpful and did what they could to get us back on the road. After he looked at the engine, he concluded it was a break in the brake line. We did what we could to fix it out in the middle of the Utah desert and drove to the next gas station to seek help. So much for a problem-free trip at Christmas time. The mechanic did what he could and we were soon on the road again after a restless night.

Everything was going well until we crossed the California border and Jewel was driving again when suddenly, the motorhome made a horrible noise, so I told Jewel to pull over slowly and stop. What was amazing is that there was a rest area to pull off on when this happened. After stopping the vehicle, we all got out to see what the problem was. Unfortunately, the right wheels had locked up and caused a small fire under the motorhome. Fortunately, our propane was turned off, which could have caused an explosion. A California Highway Patrol officer pulled up and asked what the problem was. He offered to make an appointment for us in Daggat and called for a large tow truck to get us there. He was truly a blessing that helped us get back on the road.

Daggat was about 40 miles away but did have a service station with a mechanic on the scene. After loading the motorhome on this large flatbed tow truck, we continued our journey west toward San Bernardino, CA. Daggat was a small place with a restaurant, gas station and several goats. It wasn't much but beggars cannot be choosers. We ended up spending three days in the exciting metropolis of Daggat, CA, with friendly goats for our entertainment. It was probably the most excitement they had seen in months. All of us were glad to say goodbye to Daggat, continue on our journey to San Berdu, and celebrate Christmas with the Jordan family. That is one place we will never forget but at least they were able to fix the motorhome for $1000. "Yep, on the road again." We were all glad to get moving again and land at the Jordan's for Christmas. It was time to move on and press forward to better things ahead.

Boulder-Bolder 10K Race

Every Memorial Day in Boulder, Colorado, is a fun-filled 10K race for joggers and walkers. When I was jogging on a regular basis, we would drive up to Boulder, Colorado and do this race. Boulder is located about 80 miles away from Colorado Springs. This meant we would have to get up early to drive the 80 miles up I25 until Highway 36 turned off towards Boulder. Many times, there was lots of traffic on Highway 36 because of the popular race. 40,000 – 50,000 crazy people would enter this race that made its way through downtown and neighborhoods, ending up at the University of Colorado's football stadium.

You had to register early for this race and receive your number and placement in the race. Because there are so many people, they had it broken down into A, AA, B, BB, C. CC slots all the way through the end of the alphabet. The A group was for the fastest runners and the Z group was for the slowest joggers/walkers. This helped with starting 1,000 people at a time rather than everyone at once. I remember once being scheduled to run in the CC group. Unfortunately, the traffic was so bad that I did not get to the starting gate on time. The weather was raining and I had Marsha drive as close as we could to the starting point but I still ran for a mile to enter the race. As I was running towards the starting gate, one of my colleagues yelled, "Dave, join this group." This was my CC assignment two blocks from the start. I quickly started running with the group and the 10K race ended up being a mile further for me.

Another time, Marsha and our twins were in the race along with Brooke. Marsha took some extra strength Excedrin due to getting a migraine right before the race, which made her feel extra strong. She was a trooper with blisters on her toes from running down the hill during training. We came to the conclusion that she needs to do this before every race.

There are all kinds of people in this race. I believe we were in the PP group this time. We commented it was fun to join the Porta Potty group. Speaking of Porta Potties, there are probably 100 Porta Potties for the runners to use before the race at the starting gate on race day. Because of the heat, some of the homes we ran past would be kind enough to shoot their sprinklers on the street to cool runners off. We also encountered a group from the University of Colorado dressed up like frogs. In addition to jogging, this group would be hopping over each other to add fun to their run. They obviously were in good shape to do this.

One of the big surprises of the race was the last half mile. The hill comes just when you think you only have another mile left to run. In order to enter the University of Colorado football stadium, there was a significant hill climb that tested all of us joggers. After you finished climbing the hill, it felt good to enter the stadium and finish on a flat oval track. There were lots of bystanders in the bleachers to encourage you to finish. All in all, it was a good experience and lots of fun. You really felt good when you accomplished reaching another goal.

First Family Cruise

For Jewel's graduation from high school in 1993 from Air Academy High School, we decided to treat the family to a cruise out of Miami, Florida. It was a three-day cruise on the Carnivale Carnival cruise line. It was an older ship and this was its final voyage and our room was on the bottom of the ship. We all had bunk beds for our sleeping quarters in a very small room. This was still an expensive trip but we had a good time anyway.

I ended up getting diarrhea on this cruise, which made it very uncomfortable, and Marsha was loaded up with Dramamine to combat sea sickness. Our three angels outdid us by getting a severe sunburn. They were sun tanning on the upper deck next to a man who had a dark tan and was using oil without any sun protection. They thought they would get a beautiful tan if they used the same oil as this man. As a result, all three girls got painful sunburns in areas where they had not seen the sun for a long time. They wanted an instant suntan and they got a big surprise. So that night, we bought Aloe, solar Caine and anything else that might help with their sunburns.

Unfortunately, we had tickets to attend Disney World for the next several days. This did not thrill the girls but we already had our tickets and a place to stay next to Disney World. You can imagine what the girls were thinking and saying, "We can't go on any rides as we will be bumping into our tender sunburns." But there was no turning back and we went to Disney World and had a great time. All the medication we put on the sunburns worked magic. Thank you Lord, for bringing quick healing to our angels.

I should also mention that since our ship left Miami, Florida, we were blessed with numerous teens who had just graduated from high school. Back then, there was no requirement to have at least one adult 21 years old in each room. These young people got drunk and were sicker than beached seals the next day. So much for a tranquil cruise trip.

Air Force Academy Jump School

Call me "crazy," but one thing I wanted to do in life was to jump out of a perfectly good airplane. People who understand this wild craving would say, "There is no such thing as a perfectly good airplane." Since Marsha and I had been sponsoring Air Force cadets since 1990, I was keenly aware of the jump school at the Air Force Academy (AFA). Plus as a chaplain, I thought it would be nice to have Jump Wings on my uniform underneath the cross. I felt that having jump wings on my uniform could aid in ministering to many airmen. Normally, the pilots would stay away from chaplains because they are self-sufficient and don't need any help from God. However, a chaplain who went through their jump school could break the ice and have something in common with them.

Not only did I acquire great examples of faith when going through the jump school, but being in class with cadets, I could earn their respect. I found this was true while going through the jump school course and in my future ministry with numerous airmen and women. My jump wings would often break the ice in a conversation with others. Because of the strenuous demands of the jump school course, anyone who finished the course successfully was respected. In order to qualify to enter the class, you had to pass a rigorous physical test of ten clean chin-ups, 30 clean push-ups, 20 leg lifts going from the right side to the left side and back again for core strength, and jogging a mile at nine minutes or less. During this test, 35 percent of applicants were eliminated.

Once in the course, the training was physically and mentally challenging. There was 40 hours of intense ground training to prepare you for a successful parachute landing fall (PLF). We were the last class on August 7, 1994, to use the old round parachutes. They were a real challenge since you did not have much control of them in heavy winds. Therefore, you need to practice landing forward, backward and going left or right, depending on the wind. We also had to learn what to do if we ended up landing in trees, power lines or the water, as there were all three of these elements at the AFA. We practiced in a tall building to simulate falling at 17 feet per second in lots of gravel. I bruised more parts of my body than I ever thought possible. I had cadets ask me, "Chaplain, why are you doing this?" I answered, "If I can do this at 46, you can make it too."

The last piece of the ground training simulated how to unhook from your parachute, dragging you in the winds. In order to do this, we were laying on the ground attached to our parachute and being pulled by a vehicle to imitate the wind. It required you to reach up quickly and release your parachute before being dragged too far. There was also training in what to do if your parachute line gets tangled up and doesn't open or if it partially opens. There were also various other scenarios that simulated problems with the parachute not opening properly. Then, instructions were to use your reserve parachute if all else fails.

The training at the AFA jump school course was excellent. Because of such good instruction, there have never been any fatalities at this jump school. It is also the only jump school in the world where all your jumps are free fall. Unlike the Army there is no attachment that pulls your parachute to open when jumping out of the airplane. You have been schooled to pull your rip cord to open your parachute after ten seconds. The safety rule is that if you don't pull your chute by 15 seconds, you are automatically disqualified from the course. This happened to me when, during my first jump, I pulled the rip cord at 15.5 seconds. So I had to come back and take the course again but this time, I passed it. On my first jump, I was tumbling through the air, seeing blue, green, blue, green or sky, ground, sky, ground. I was so thankful for my parachute opening up and I said, "Thank you, God."

In this course, you are literally putting your life in the hands of the skilled people who pack your parachute. This is the first part of learning about faith. Then the second is when you step out in faith and leave the airplane, hoping your parachute will open. The last step of faith comes when you pull the rip cord to open up your parachute. You are so glad when it loudly pops open and gives you a strong jolt up in your body. They say this feeling is equivalent to four Gs but it feels so good and you don't mind this uncomfortable pull. You are safe once again and preparing to have a safe landing and not hit your head on the ground. This whole experience was well worth it.

While David was at the jump school jumping out of airplanes, I got a call from USAF Hospital asking for Mrs. Markwalder. "Yes, this is she." We are calling you to notify you that your biopsy from melanoma came back malignant.

I answered, "OH Good!" she answered, "That's not the reaction I usually get." I told her, "My husband is at the Jump School at AFA so I'm glad your call wasn't about him." she totally understood. Although my family thought I was a bit nuts in going through this course, I knew it was something I needed to do. In order to take this class, you need to have a physical approving your health. The doctor told me, "Your physical health is great but I question your mental health in wanting to do this."

Blizzard of 1997

It was in October 1997 that a surprise Ice Storm was going to cripple the state of Colorado. I was still a chaplain in the Air Force and stationed at Lowry Air Force Base in Denver. I was commuting from Colorado Springs to Denver and leaving at 5:30 am to arrive at work by 7:30 am. The traffic was quite heavy because of road work in the southern part of Denver and it would take 1 ¾ -2 hours to drive to work. Fortunately, I had at least 1-3 carpool friends who also lived in the Springs or Monument.

However, I will be driving alone in our little white Geo Metro this morning because I have to attend a retirement dinner for one of our enlisted airmen. The morning started out like most other mornings, with heavy traffic but no snow or rain. Then it happened a strong snowstorm crept into the whole state of Colorado and by the time I was to leave work, I was faced with a heavy snowstorm. The retirement dinner should have been postponed but because it wasn't, I went from work to the restaurant in Lakewood. Marsha even called me and warned me of a perfect storm that was heading our way.

I normally would have skipped the dinner and headed home but my boss was already mean-spirited and did not like me so I couldn't afford to give him another reason to write me up. The ridiculous thing about this is when I got to the retirement dinner, several of my co-workers did not show because of the dangerous snowstorm. They had gone home to Denver and decided not to attend it. But I went the extra mile and took the higher road and attended the function. The event was quite nice but should have been postponed for a week. I blame my boss for his poor leadership and not making a good decision.

After dinner, I made a good choice and stopped at a gas station on the way to I25 to fill up the gas. This was an excellent decision for what I was about to face in the next 12 hours. As I drove towards the freeway to drive home, I noticed that the freeway was completely stopped with 100s of cars at the Lincoln on-ramp. So, I decided to drive over the freeway and take the back route home on Highway 83. Then I discovered a complete whiteout just ½ mile down the road and decided to turn around and go back to the crowded freeway. Driving a white Geo Metro in a whiteout was too risky and I would probably become stranded. So I returned to the freeway and joined the other 400 cars and 18-wheel trucks waiting for the traffic to start to move again. We all thought there was probably an accident ahead at Happy Canyon, which frequently has fender benders.

I turned the radio on to AM 850 KOA, which has the most current and accurate news but was not reporting any accidents on I-25 at Happy Canyon. This was not your typical snowstorm but an ice storm with extreme winds and a temperature of 0 degrees. So I sat in the car, hoping that the traffic would start to move any minute. I joined this parking lot of cars at around 10 pm and it was currently midnight and still no movement. I listened to the radio again but they only reported that there were 100s of cars stuck at the Lincoln exit but no mention of the freeway being closed because of this ice storm. If I had known that the road was closed earlier, I could have gone back to Lincoln exit on the ramp, driven back to Denver, and found a warm place to stay that night. By the time the radio station reported that the I-25 was closed, it was 2 am in the morning and the snow was too high for me to get back to Denver.

Fortunately, I was wearing a turtleneck and had my gym bag with a pair of tennis shoes in it that I put on. I also had a quilt blanket in the back that I used to put over my head to keep my body heat in. It was so cold that I had to turn on the car every hour to heat it up and go outside to make sure the exhaust pipe was not covered up and the tires were free from the ice, still hoping to move. Finally, at 3:00 am, I fell asleep with the blanket over my head. I woke up at 6:30 am, my teeth chattering and my body shaking. I was extremely cold and got the heater on.

I decided to get out of the car and check everything. I walked up to the car behind me to see how the driver was doing. I asked him how his gas gauge was and he said it was almost empty. I said, "Why don't you join me in my car as I have plenty of gas and we can use my heater. Plus, the body heat from two people in a small car would also help." he agreed to the offer and for the next seven hours we had a lot of good conversions in the midst of a challenging situation.

Finally, at noon, there were Denver residents who heard about our plight and came out to try and help us. At first, they walked by all the cars and offered food and water, which was a gift. Then those people who had 4-wheel drive trucks and a heavy-duty chain came up with the plan to have one car at a time run across the medium (20' wide) as far as you could and then put a chain around the front bumper and pull you to the other side so you could drive back to Denver on the freeway. It took two hours before it was my turn to try and get across the medium and head back to Denver.

My car buddy said goodbye, and each of us got into our vehicles to be rescued by these angels of mercy. When I made it across the medium and started heading north towards Denver, I got off the freeway when I spotted a nearby grocery store. I parked the car and went inside the store and the first thing I noticed was how warm it was in the store. I thanked God for the warmth and for the telephone that was located on the side of the wall. Back in 1997, we did not have any cell phones so I was not able to call Marsha all night long and tell her of my predicament. It was a good phone call and put her at ease with my situation. She then called our deputy chaplain, David Cornthwaite, and he came to the grocery store. I followed him to his home, where I slept overnight since the freeway was still closed. David was a Christian Scientist and was a very empathetic man. In fact, he told me, "I don't know what Father Doyle has against you but for some reason, he has it out for you." He told me he had written a stellar Officer Performance Report on me that Father Doyle chose not to use. He was determined to damage my career as an Air Force Officer. Ultimately, God interceded and placed a colonel who knew me personally and of my sterling record on the promotion board to colonel. Another example of "When God shows up."

Jewel and Christian's Wedding
June 6, 1998

A few years before their wedding date, a dozen roses were delivered to our front door for Jewel. We teased her by saying, "So, who is this boyfriend sending you roses." Jewel answered, "He is just a friend. Nothing serious." A few months later, when a couple of Jewel's girlfriends from Wheaton College were visiting, we asked them if there was anything serious with this guy and they said "YES." You would get two opposite answers when you ask Jewel to explain her dating with Christian and then ask Christian the same question. It's like they are in different worlds.

After several of Christian's visits with Jewel to Colorado Springs, Christian asked Marsha and me if he could meet privately with us the next morning. Having been raised with proper etiquette in Green Bay, Wisconsin, he told us that he loved Jewel and asked if he could have her hand in marriage. We responded with a resounding "YES." This set things in motion for a June 6 wedding the following year in 1998. This was exactly one year after they had graduated from Wheaton College in Wheaton, Illinois.

Jewel and Christian both attended Wheaton College and were both Communication majors. This is how they met. This was a long way for us to drive from Colorado Springs so Jewel only came home while in college on major holidays like Thanksgiving, Christmas and Spring break. When Jewel visited Wheaton College as a senior in high school, the taxi from the airport dropped her off a mile from her lodging area. Unfortunately, there was snow and freezing rain that she had to walk in. This was not a good start to Wheaton College but God wanted to attend there and in spite of the bad weather, she decided to go there. This is how she met Christian and the rest is history.

Once the question had been asked, it set the wedding plans in motion. There were numerous items to cover before the wedding could take place. Some of the major ones were the decision on the invitations, list of who to invite, where to get married, where the reception takes place, what kind of cake, what kind of meal to serve at the reception, tuxes to rent, bridal dress to choose, bride maids dresses, mother of the bride's dress, place for the dress rehearsal dinner and program, and the list goes on. It was like planning a major conference.

Jewel and Christian also needed to pick out a minister. They chose Mateen Elaas, a minister at First Presbyterian Church in Colorado Springs, where they married. The reception was held at the Sheraton Hotel in Colorado Springs, which I had reserved for several Air Force Chaplains' conferences over the past couple of years. I found the personnel at the hotel very professional and the facility pristine. When I asked about having the reception there, they were very congenial and gave us a discount and excellent service. This allowed us to have two ice sculptures and a spacious dance floor. The meal was delicious and everyone who came had a good time. Although the wedding took place on "D-Day," this was a joyous occasion.

Recruiting Chaplain Candidates and Chaplains

My job as an Air Force Chaplain was absolutely the best. I was privileged to recruit Chaplain Candidates and Reserve Chaplains to become important resources for the Air Force Chaplain Service. Chaplain Candidates are full-time students who are in seminary studying to become ministers, priests or rabbis. In this mission, I would travel throughout the United States and visit seminaries to talk with students about becoming a chaplain candidate. The Air Force gave me the authority to offer a qualified student $4,000 to help pay for their tuition per year. This did not pay for their full tuition but certainly helped.

The qualified students would be 2nd Lieutenants in the Air Force and get full pay plus a housing allowance while doing summer training. This would happen in between semesters and be a great summer job while finishing their schooling. Once they graduated from seminary with a Master of Divinity degree, they could become a 1st Lieutenant and be a Reserve or Active Duty chaplain. This would be the beginning of a valuable career in the military to help personnel who might be struggling in their career and to encourage the morale of the airmen.

Chaplains are crucial for the success of any mission, and they can greatly support any commander in leading their troops in war and peace. Many airmen will not go to a mental health provider for fear that it may negatively impact their career but will talk with a chaplain because of the code of confidentiality. This is a special gift given to the chaplain core, which allows chaplains to have an open-door policy that airmen respect.

Because my recruiting was for both Chaplain Candidates and Reserve Chaplains, it also catapulted the scope of influence to active-duty chaplains. During my time of recruiting, Total Force in the military became a huge theme. The active duty realized during the war that their troops were stretched too thin and could not accomplish the mission without the aid of Reservists. Therefore, many Reserve Chaplains were called to active duty to support the critical needs of the Air Force. Numerous active-duty chaplains were deployed to the war zone, leaving the home bases without adequate chaplain support. This is where Reserve Chaplains played an invaluable part in filling the needs at home.

My job allowed me to go to seminaries and colleges and share my story of the Air Force Chaplain Service with interested college and graduate students. It was a delight to rub shoulders and meet sharp students who were very excited about entering the ministry. Not only did I recruit Protestant chaplains, but Catholic Priests, Jewish Rabbis, and Muslim Iman's. I was called to recruit people of all faiths to support the various faiths of military personnel. I traveled to Chicago, Boston, San Francisco, Los Angeles, Phoenix, Cincinnati, Atlanta and many other large cities where college and seminary students were studying. In addition, I led a 30-member Reserve Chaplain recruiting team that multiplied my recruiting efforts through-out the United States. We met together every year to train and equip ourselves for the mission. My main focus was "to shape the future of the Air Force Chaplaincy." What a great calling and privilege to accomplish this fabulous task.

Visit to Chanelle in Germany 2001

It was 2001, and Chanelle had been working in Germany with Military Communities with Young Life and Youth for Christ at two Air Force bases. Her responsibility was to focus on the youth at Spangdahlem and Bitberg AFB. She had been there for a year when we decided to visit her as a family. Jewel and Christian had been married for almost three years and lived in Chicago for Christian's work. Starlene lived in Florida doing graduate work in psychology and would fly from there. The plan was for each of us to fly from our different destinations and meet up in Germany. All was going well until we received a phone call from Star saying she did not have a ticket two hours before she was supposed to fly out. We told her to buy one just to get over there. Unfortunately, they sold her a one-way ticket. When we met David and Kimberly Unruh at the airport in Germany, they helped us find an inexpensive ticket for Star to fly home. He was stationed there in the Air Force. It is so nice to meet a familiar face when you are in a foreign land.

After we got over that mishap, the rest of the trip went extremely well. Chanelle rented a small Renault minivan through the Air Force Base for us to get around in. Starlene was a great sport and sat in the far back with the entire luggage. We planned to be with Chanelle for a week and visit our Swiss relatives in Zurich, Switzerland, several hours south of the Black Forest where Chanelle was living. Chanelle was able to purchase gas coupons at the base, which saved us money.

So we loaded ourselves into the small van and were off for a memorable road trip. Marsha and I hadn't seen our Swiss relatives since 1973, after I graduated from Seminary. We had stayed with them for two weeks and had a wonderful visit when I was 25, and Marsha was 24. It was now 28 years later and we had a fabulous visit with them. We were only planning on staying there two days but when they said if you stay one more day, we will fix you an authentic Swiss Fondue dinner, so we agreed. How can one turn down such a generous offer. The meal was definitely worth staying for.

The next day, we left and headed to the famous castle, Neuschwanstein. It is the one that Walt Disney copied for Disneyland and Disney World. Every so often we would get lost when driving on the back roads. This one time, I said I think we need to stop and find out where we are. It was a small Ma and Pa store that Jewel and I went in to get directions. I said in English with my best broken German accent if they spoke English. When I did not get a positive response, I repeated it with using my hands and speaking slower and louder. Finally, Jewel bailed me out since she had minored in German in college and spent two months in the summer in Germany and Switzerland learning German. This was good for a laugh and Jewel spoke good enough German to communicate to these Germans who did not speak any English.

We had lots of fun driving on back roads but through some beautiful scenery. It was definitely an adventure finding new restaurants to eat at and hotels to stay for the night. We were winging it but enjoying every minute of time together. In fact, when Christian was asked what part of the trip he enjoyed the most, he said, "Riding in the van." He really got a firsthand glimpse of who our family is and how we enjoy life. There was one part of the ride when Marsha evidently called him Carl instead of Christian. She doesn't remember it, but to this day, he still teases her about it. Jewel said there was also a time when Christian asked Jewel if we were going to stop for lunch. Jewel answered, "My dad has trail mix to hold us over." Obviously, Christian was not used to this kind of traveling. But he was a great sport and survived.

Another time, we got on the German auto bond where there is no speed limit, and people travel over 100 mph, and Chanelle said, "Dad, you need to get over in the right lane." I was going 80 mph and thought I was safe with nobody behind me. Suddenly, someone whipped passed us in the left lane. They came from nowhere. That was quite an experience. This was one fabulous trip being with Chanelle, meeting our Swiss relatives that our children had never met, and traveling in the minivan.

Pentagon Assignment Post 9/11

The common question to everyone is, "Where were you when 9/11 happened?" I was recruiting Air Force Chaplains in the San Francisco area when I heard over the radio that one of the Twin Towers in New York had been hit by a passenger plane and was on fire. At first, I thought it was an advertisement for a new movie that was being released. It seemed so surreal that I thought it was not really happening. Then, reality sunk in, and this was not fiction but really occurring. It was hard to comprehend that one human being would be so evil and actually do such a horrific action. It just was not common sense and I did not want to believe it. But we soon learned this was happening and the unthinkable was reality. This was a new form of terrorism that no one could have imagined.

As a result of 9/11, I was called up to serve at the Pentagon and assist in deploying active-duty chaplains to Afghanistan as part of a crisis action team (CAT). But I later discovered the real reason I was at the Pentagon post 9/11 was to offer a "ministry of presence" to scores of people. At this time, only one full-time Army chaplain was assigned to the Pentagon for over 20,000 people. To support this monster building was a humongous parking lot where I had to walk a full mile to reach the edifice. The Pentagon at this time was like a war zone, and it did not know if there were going to be more surprise attacks. The military had machine guns posted on the roof and high security at all entrances. This was an extremely stressful time to be assigned there, and a chaplain's presence was very important when visiting and praying with people.

In addition, there were surprise deliveries to our Congressmen of Anthrax, a poisonous white powder that was very harmful. When I visited Congressman Joel Hefley from Colorado, I asked him how I might pray for you and the nation. He paused and said, "David, you are the first person asking to pray in my office. There is much fear in our nation as we have never faced terrorism hitting America at home before. Please pray for wisdom and safety during this difficult time." I did pray and he really appreciated it. This was a dark time for America and a time when they desperately needed God's help.

When I got to the Pentagon, I went around to the area where the commercial airplane had hit the side of the building. It was hard for me to conceive as I thought this was truly evil personified. How could one individual do this to another? The huge gaping hole in the side of the Pentagon was horrific and a reminder of the evil that hovers in our world. The misguided thinking that committing such a tragedy was following the will of Allah is irrational and distorted thinking. The only silver lining on this tragic event that killed 192 people is the airplane struck the exact place in the Pentagon that was under reconstruction. Normally, there would have been another 1,000 people working in that area. Because this area was still being worked on, it was vacant. As a result of the new construction, it was much stronger than any other area in the Pentagon and kept the airplane from going further into the building.

Many people ask the question, "Where was God when 9/11 occurred?" Although almost 3,000 people were killed in this terrorist attack, it could have been much worse. If the attack had happened one hour later, there would have been thousands more in the twin towers who would have died. The fact that the first tower stayed up so long, allowed many people to escape. The fourth flight that was aimed at hitting the capital building was fortunately stopped by brave passengers and crashed in Pennsylvania. Plus, the Pentagon attack could have been much worse, as mentioned earlier.

In the months after 9/11 I spent in the Pentagon, I had the privilege of ministering to many men and women who were afraid and did not know if there would be more terrorist attacks in Washington, DC. There was a spirit of fear that permeated the air following 9/11. When I visited a Security Policeman on Thanksgiving protecting the Pentagon, he asked me to pray for him and his colleagues and their families who were concerned for these soldiers' safety. It was a unique time in the history of our capital that America had never faced before. I felt blessed to be able to bring these soldiers and civilians some peace in the midst of chaos, reminding them that God was ultimately in charge of this situation.

Flunked Retirement Again

After 26 years as an Air Force Chaplain and 32 years in the ministry as a Presbyterian Minister, I retired from active duty in the Air Force. My last assignment was at Warner Robins Air Force Base in Georgia. This was located 100 miles south of Atlanta and its fame to claim is it was just south of the gnat line. When the sun began to set, plenty of gnats came out to bless you with their presents. You could tell the difference between a newbie and an established resident. The newbie would try to swat the gnats with their hands in front of their face. The old-time resident would simply blow them away with a heavy burst of air past their nostrils.

Before my retirement in November 2006, Marsha and I lived for three or four years in Warner Robins. We discovered what heavy humidity was all about. We got up early every morning to do yard work only to discover incredible heat was already upon us. After working for 30 minutes, we had to shake out our sun glasses that were dripping from our perspiration. We also learned that we needed to visit Atlanta if we wanted any true culture. Marsha felt like she was doing real estate sitting on her head because it was so backward. There was also a "good old boy club" that was quite evident in the real estate field. Besides a good job of recruiting chaplain candidates and reserve chaplains in the Air Force, I enjoyed a line dancing club that we belonged to every week. This was good exercise and fun.

After my retirement from the Air Force, I was unemployed for ten months while trying to discern what I wanted to do next. Finally, it became obvious that I should go back to the civilian ministry, and I became an interim pastor at Faith Presbyterian Church from October 2007 to May 2008. I enjoyed the new job following an interim pastor who was only there for six months. I later found out that Art Bell would only stay at a church for six months and then it was time to move on. When I came to the church, it was still suffering from a new pastor from Florida who had only served at Faith Pres for seven months. His wife never came out here with him which was a clear sign that his short term was imminent. This short-term left a sour taste in the congregation and caused them to be gun shy of any future pastor. My first several months there was to build trust in my pastorate from a broken congregation that needed healing. After eight months as an interim pastor, I completed my mission, and a new pastor was selected. Marsha and I said our good-byes and left after a positive experience with this church. We made many new friends in this congregation and it wasn't easy to leave.

As soon as I left this church, I heard about a small Presbyterian Church on the west side of Colorado Springs called Gateway Pres that was seeking a new pastor. Unfortunately, the church had a bad split when their former pastor left and damage was rampant. There was a need for a new pastor to come and bring healing to this congregation, similar to Faith Pres I just left. I put my dossier together and submitted it. The next week, the search committee called to meet with me, so I went for an interview. After discussing the main issues and coming to an agreement on the salary, they called me to be their next pastor. Unfortunately, the next day, the chairman of the committee called me and told me they could not afford the salary they offered me. Because I felt called to help this congregation, I met with the chairperson the next day and came to an agreement that I would accept a lower salary package in exchange for two more weeks of study leave so I could pursue my Doctor of Ministry degree.

Although I told the hiring committee that I would be there for 3- four years to bring them stability, I ended up staying for seven years until June 2015. I was now 67 years old and I had served in the Presbyterian Church for 41 years and I felt it was time to retire. I thoroughly enjoyed my seven years of ministry and witnessed many people growing in their faith. Plus, when Marsha and I came there, the church only had an average attendance of 50-60 people. The "A" team (Dave and Marsha) rolled up our sleeves and brought new life into this congregation with the amazing help of God's Spirit. One of the first things we did was to recruit 35 volunteers to help out on a Saturday morning yard day to bring pride back in the despicable church yard. It was so bad the neighboring church thought Gateway was closed. By the time we were finished and I retired in 2015, the average attendance was now 120-130 and we enjoyed a church yard and parking lot that we could be proud of and was a positive witness in the neighborhood.

After enjoying a couple of months off, I received a phone call from Gary Weaver, who was the Presbytery Executive. He asked me to consider helping out at First Presbyterian Church in Pueblo because both of the previous interim pastors only lasted 4-5 months each and he was helping out during the gap for the second time and was burned out. He told me I would start in November and it would only last for three months as they had two possible candidates that the search committee had lined up. I told him, "but Gary, I just retired." he said, "I know that is why I am calling you to help out. This church is in desperate need of healing and calmness and you are the man who can do it." After praying about it and discussing it with Marsha, I met with their session and accepted the offer. Marsha told me she is not cut out to be a part of an Interim position as it is too hard to say good-bye after a short stint and she would not be joining me. This only lasted one week and she graciously joined me in this new, exciting venture. I agreed to the salary and commute to Pueblo four times a week 55 miles each way.

God gave me the strength to do this demanding ministry to a church with two services: contemporary at 8:30 am and traditional at 11:00 am. First Pres in Pueblo was a larger congregation with 130-150 people in the early service and 175-200 in the traditional service. The staff was hurting and needed a shepherd to come alongside them and give them confidence and love. After a few months, I saw a wonderful, positive change in attitude in the staff. Unfortunately, a month after I started, the search committee got the notice that both of the potential candidates were no longer interested and had accepted other positions. When I met with the search committee, a dark cloud permeated the room. I told them, "I know you are very disappointed but this is God's church and He still has the right new pastor for you to find. I will be here in this process until you complete your mission." This helped bring a calmness that was critical for the committee to proceed.

One of the joys that Marsha and I had was to be invited to join the Praise team at the contemporary service. She played her violin, and I played my guitar next to that of a good guitarist. This was a stretching but rewarding part of our ministry in Pueblo. Instead of staying for three months, I ended up serving there for nine months until August 2016. During these nine months, I saw God's marvelous hand blessing the ministry. Not only did the attendance in the church grow, but I was also able to help them develop a fellowship committee, Christian Education committee, and worship committee, which were desperately needed to lead the church. We also witnessed a great healing in the church from people being angry and divided to wholeness and unity. First Pres Pueblo was definitely a different church at the end of my tenure than when we first came. God's Spirit did a great work. To God be the Glory!! One of the bonuses was we enjoyed going out to lunch every Sunday with many of the members.

In September 2022, when you think your ministry is finally finished after being retired for six years (2016-2022), I received a call from my good friend Bob Leivers, who was the new Presbytery Executive. He asked me if I would be interested in helping First Pres Church in Pueblo since there Senior Pastor was retiring on November 6, 2022. They needed a pastor to preach and lead worship for five Sundays in Advent beginning November 27. I would only have to fill the pulpit and drive down there once a week. I talked to Marsha and we prayed about it and God seemed to say yes, so I agreed to do this, receiving $150 each week plus travel expenses. It was like God said, "Now that I healed you, I need you back in the saddle to help with ministry. You are now competent to do this, so go forth." This experience was another positive event in our lives as this congregation filled up our love cups. What a great opportunity to serve God and witness a congregation that needed healing and calmness. There was much anxiety and worry about their future. Through God's Spirit, I was able to alleviate much fear. We even witnessed the start of a revival as new life came back into this church. Praise God!!!

Keiths After Chuck's death

After Chuck died in December 2006, we all felt betrayed as we were supposed to grow old together. We hoped for many more memorable dinners and time with the Keith family. Instead, Chuck surprised us all by suddenly dyeing. We knew Chuck had a serious weight problem and was obese, but we thought he was under the doctor's care and still doing well. I wanted to spend many more days and time together with Chuck, not be part of the memorial service in honor of him. This just did not seem right. He was a positive person that made you feel good when around him. Chuck had a great sense of humor and kept us laughing with his sayings. But now we were dealing with a widow, Domie, in deep grief. She was in shock from Chuck's death and was wondering how she and her family were going to be able to handle life without him.

Fortunately, Chuck was a very organized person and left a binder with all the details of funeral arrangements, finances, and other important details that would be overwhelming without specific direction from him. It was almost as if he knew his death could be imminent and he did not want to bring unnecessary confusion and grief after he died. He gave Domie and his family a great gift with directions for his life insurance policies, clear will with his wishes, and other important items to free the family from making hard decisions. The emotional grief process is difficult enough without adding the stress of the unknown finances, will, medical power of attorney, and the overwhelming items that happen with death. When we were there with Domie, she pulled out the book that Chuck had prepared and gave specific directions to aid Domie with life insurance policies and who to contact to assist her with finances. What a huge blessing this was and it took the pressure off of her to know that she was going to be alright financially after Chuck's death. Although Domie said, "This is all good but I would rather have Chuck be here instead." Being organized like this was the next best thing that Chuck could have done for his family to help them get through this big loss. Chuck provided a solid foundation for his family to help them carry on in life. This was certainly Chuck's wish for his family to be strong together in their future journey. What an incredible gift to his family, who are still strong and together today.

After a few years as a widow, Domie saw the need to create a support group for widows at her church, Saddleback Community Church, with Pastor Rick Warren. At first, it wasn't easy to begin a new group like this but now, years later, she is the leader of three strong widow's groups who meet every month. These groups have helped numerous widows get through the hard time of losing a spouse and facing loneliness. Domie has taken the positive stance of helping other widows like herself get through life rather than feeling sorry for herself. Domie has become a regular attender of Saddleback Community Church and has joined the choir and will be singing in five services this Easter 2023. We have witnessed a change in this lady who came from France as a nominal Catholic to an all-out committed Christian who is serving God using her talents.

Trip to Yellowstone National Park

On August 23, 2011, we finally got to visit Yellowstone National Park. We had wanted to do this for many years and it became a reality in 2011. We had been told that you could rent trailers at campsites through the Air Force for a very reasonable rate. I checked into it and discovered that it was $80 a night, which was doable in contrast to staying at nearby hotels, which were twice as much. The key is you had to make your reservation a year in advance through Mountain Home Air Force Base in Idaho for Yellowstone Country Trailers. We stayed there for seven days and enjoyed the serene experience of camping in the great outdoors in a beautiful setting. Since we were located inside the national park, everything we wanted to see was close by. It was a 25-foot trailer that was perfect for the two of us. We enjoyed the quietness and intimacy of being alone. Perfect for a romantic vacation for two.

For the next six days, we enjoyed seeing the many sights and sounds that Yellowstone National Park had to offer. One of the surprises that was not on our to-do list was when I got pulled over by a Park Ranger for going too fast. I was going down a long, straight-a-way and our Chrysler 300m picked up speed and a red light flashed in my rear view mirror as Marsha said, "David, you are going too fast." Oh no, I thought. What was I doing wrong? When this pretty, young officer pulled me over, she asked me if I was aware that there was a 45 miles per hour (mph) maximum speed limit in the national park? I answered "NO." There were no speed limit signs, but I was going 60 mph by the time I reached the bottom of the hill. I apologized to the officer and then she took my license, registration and insurance and went back to her car for a long time. I thought, "Oh boy, she is going to throw the book at me." When she finally returned, she said, "I am only going to give you a warning this time. Please slowdown in our park." Wow, I felt relieved. I thanked her and then Marsha said, "I want you to treat us to an expensive dinner at the restaurant overlooking the lake and tall Tetons." I told her that was a deal. I would much rather pay for a best-ever dinner than a traffic ticket.

We saw many fascinating things, including watching "Old Faithful" shoot up with a massive amount of steam in a regular time pattern. This was not the only geyser in the park but it was definitely the most famous for its regularity. We also saw a large herd of buffalo grazing in one of the many meadows. It is amazing how big these creatures are and the damage they can do to humans. The park was good about warning people to be very cautious around them. There was also the hotel where Teddy Roosevelt stayed when he established

Yellowstone as a National Park. I was surprised at how many miles you could travel through-out the park. We learned Yellowstone is the oldest national park in the United States.

Marsha and I thoroughly enjoyed our visit to Yellowstone National Park and we would like to visit it again with our family. Right next to Yellowstone is The Grand Tetons National Park, which is incredible as well. It has high, jagged mountains and pristine lakes to capture your attention. We enjoyed driving through this park as well. However, it is much smaller than Yellowstone and less to visit.

Chanelle and Carlos's Wedding

Sept 15, 2012

After years of college, missionary work in Germany, and attending graduate school, Chanelle found the right person to marry. They had dated for several months when Carlos visited us in Colorado. We were talking with Carlos in the family room when I could tell he was nervous. So, I asked him what his plans were for their future relationship. Carlos then popped the question asking for our permission to marry Chanelle. This was a joyful time to celebrate their relationship. They decided they wanted to get married in Bishop, California, on September 15, 2012.

Now that the plan was in motion, they had about six months to arrange all the plans and make it a reality. This included finding a church, looking for a reception place, planning the meal at the reception, ordering the invitations, making a list of people to invite, choosing the cake, reserving the hotel rooms in Bishop, shopping at various stores to get the best deal, and many other details. I have always said that planning a wedding is like putting together a major conference. We helped in areas like sending out invitations, table decorations and name tags for the tables.

I remember packing our small Prius to the hilt with all the sparkling cider bottles, decorations for the tables, and numerous other items, not to mention our personal suitcases. Our Prius was brand new, and this was our first major road trip. We were very pleased that it ran smoothly and we got the incredible gas mileage of 53 miles per gallon. When we got to Bishop, we unloaded the car at our hotel. Because some family members were having financial difficulties, we offered to pay for two nights for them at the hotel. All five of them stayed in a two-bedroom room.

Besides the wedding, one of the great joys of this trip was to meet many of Carlos' family and friends. After the wedding rehearsal, Carlos' family hosted a delicious Mexican meal in the backyard of a backyard of his sister's home. We enjoyed eating a fabulous homemade meal. During the evening celebration, several people shared their joys of knowing Carlos and Chanelle. This special and intimate event prepared us for the next day's grand wedding.

I had the privilege of officiating at their wedding in a small church in Bishop. Around 150 people attended the wedding. They asked Harold Bussell, Chanelle's uncle, to assist in the wedding ceremony at the very beginning so I could walk Chanelle down the aisle and then answer the question, "Who gives this woman to be married to this man?" I responded, "Her mother and I do with great love and joy." It was a wonderful wedding ceremony and a privilege to invite God to be an important part of their lives.

After searching for a place to have their wedding reception, they unanimously decided to have it at the church's social hall. We had several round tables and decorated each with a center piece. Although the social hall was not fancy, we added decorations to make it festive. We included a space for dancing in the middle of it, which was very important. The catered meal was delicious and after cutting the cake, it was time to kick up our heals and dance. Our granddaughter, Mae Magoon, who was four years old, had lots of fun dancing until her face turned red. Many people joined the bride and groom on the dance floor. One of the fun things to witness was the questions given to Chanelle and Carlos. They needed to respond to which one of them was more outgoing, more structured, etc. It was fun to learn all about them and much humor was enjoyed. After the bride and groom left, it was time to clean-up the social hall. Fortunately, many people helped return the place clean and ready for use on Sunday. A positive and magnificent wedding celebration happened on September 15, 2012, in the quaint little town of Bishop, California.

Trip to Greece

Oct 2012

The year 2012 was filled with several major events, including a trip to Greece in October. In addition to all the regular events that fill a calendar, like Easter, Thanksgiving and Christmas, there was a major fire in Colorado Springs in June. The Waldo Canyon fire swept over the mountains and down the canyons to bring horrific destruction and the loss of over 400 homes. We were evacuated for one week during this fire, not knowing if our house would be destroyed or not. We stayed with good friends who lived downtown, away from the fire. When we were finally allowed to return to our neighborhood, we were fortunate that the fire had not affected any of the homes where we lived. It came close but was contained before doing any damage.

Besides the Waldo Canyon fire during the summer, we also were deeply involved in planning a wedding for Chanelle and Carlos. They were getting married in September in Bishop, California. Since it was not a local wedding, making plans in a location over 1000 miles away became a challenge. After the wedding, we planned to take a trip to Greece, which was part of a Pilgrimage for my Spirituality certificate from Columbia Theological Seminary in Decatur, Georgia. This had been in our plans for over a year before the fire and wedding happened.

So, a month after returning home from attending a beautiful wedding in California, it was time to change gears and get ready to attend a Pilgrimage in Greece. The trip included following the Apostle Paul's footsteps in Ephesus, Colossae,

Philippi, Thessalonica, Greece, Santorini, Turkey, and other interesting places. We were with 30 other students and spouses for a trip of a lifetime. The trip included traveling numerous miles on a bus and discovering many of the sites that Paul covered during his missionary visits. We even boarded a small passenger ship to roam the Aegean Sea and visit the island of Patmos, where the Apostle John wrote "The Revelation."

We also visited "The Hanging Monasteries" which were hundreds of feet up on the side of a cliff, giving the monks the solitude and privacy they sought. It was incredible to witness how they could have built these places. They were breath taking just to see them. But to actually live up there was unbelievable. Another site we enjoyed visiting was the river site where Paul encountered Lydia, the woman of purple. We learned that she was rich and well-off and could support the early church with her wealth. We enjoyed worshipping in a chapel on the grounds, reflecting on her story, and singing "The Doxology" in acappella, which was beautiful. Although the leader of the group was more focused on the icons of Greek Orthodox than the steps of Paul, it was still a very good trip, capturing many historic sites, including Athens and the Greek temples.

Oh Deer

It happened in one of my last years as the Pastor at Gateway Presbyterian Church in Colorado Springs. I became the pastor of this church in the summer of 2008 and retired after seven years in May 2015. This was a very good last assignment for me to serve in ministry. When I came to Gateway in 2008, the church was dysfunctional, with problems in the session and anger problems from a split in the church over the last pastor. It needed much healing and development to create a positive image of itself. There was a serious problem among the parishioners and the building and landscaping were in dire need of improvement.

When I first arrived at the church, I went across the street to introduce myself as the new pastor. The staff at the Evangelical Free Church thought Gateway Presbyterian Church was closed because the yard was so overgrown. What a poor witness this was in the neighborhood. One of the first things I did as the pastor was to challenge the members of the church to join Marsha and me for a Saturday morning yard clean-up. I was told, "Pastor, you will be lucky if you get 5-6 people to come out. On our first clean-up day, we had 30+ people who showed up and worked hard for three hours, followed by a free pizza luncheon in the fellowship hall. We filled up a large bend that we rented and took several truckloads of debris to the dump. This was an incredibly successful event and helped the people to become proud of their church grounds. The church became a positive witness for God once again. We had yard clean-up days twice a year.

When I was there several years ago, my secretary and care director came to me and said, "Pastor, there is a problem. The church has a dead deer on the grounds." They had called the humane society for dead animals but were told that the city does not remove dead animals on private property. The animal must be picked up on city property. It was going to cost the church $300 for a private company to come and get it. I asked where the deer was, and they showed me. To my surprise, it had obviously been there for several hours, if not days. It smelled terrible and was covered with flies swarming around it in the heat of the day.

Evidently, it had been hit by a car on the road next to the church and jumped over the 3' cement barrier, where it died. I told the ladies not to contact the private company to get it. I knew exactly what needed to be done. I went out there where the dead deer lay and, grabbed its two front hoofs and slung it over the cement barrier so it landed on city property. The deer must have weighed at least 100 lbs. as it took all my strength to hurl it over the barrier. The ladies marveled at what I had done and commented, "This is a new part of the pastor's job description." I told them that this reminded me of being a cowboy in Nevada when I was 16 and 17 and lifted heavy bales of hay during the summer hay season. They just shook their heads and laughed. I saved the church $300 and was a good steward of the church's finances.

Mother Going Home at 99

In contrast to Dad's sudden, unexpected death, Mother plotted along, hoping to reach 100 but falling eight months short at 99. She died on January 15, 2015, after suffering from a mild form of dementia. My younger sister, Florence, and her husband, Rich, had been caring for Mother at their home in Porterville, CA, for 20 years before she died. Mother offered to give them $30,000 so they could buy a new home and convert their third-car garage into a grandma's flat where she lived. This was an ideal arrangement, giving her a social outlet and not being isolated like she was living alone in her home in San Jose, CA, for five years after Dad died. This allowed her the flexibility of not being totally alone without being a burden on Florence and Rich. It also allowed her to travel with her sister-in-law or other friends without worrying about her home. I believe this arrangement was one of the reasons she lived to be 99 years of age.

Mother's faith was always important to her, and she joined the Jordans by attending the Nazarene Church in town. She also joined the senior citizens' exercise class to keep her mind and body in shape. She outlived her closest relatives and enjoyed celebrating with family and friends. Whenever Mother traveled, she was not afraid to see new things. Unlike my father, who was more reserved, my mother loved to be adventurous.

Mother had a deep faith and even attended a Bible college after high school. Very few women attended college in the early 1930s when mom did. She completed all four years and received a bachelor's degree. She put her education to good use and was the Women's Missionary Council president at our San Jose, CA, church for over 20 years. This was her way of being a faithful servant of God and supporting missionaries around the world. I can remember when, growing up we had missionaries over for lunch after the 11 am worship service almost every month. This was her way of taking care of people who needed a meal and showing love and hospitality. As children and youth, we did not resent it as a wonderful meal that would be enjoyed by all and give us a chance to meet new families.

I had the privilege of leading a short graveside service for my mother in San Jose, CA. That morning it rained hard. As we stood under the canopy, I said, "And they said it never rains in northern California because of a long drought they experienced." This was the beginning of the end of that drought. However, it did not put a damper on our time together, remembering a wonderful person who died. Following the graveside service, we gathered in a warm and dry room to continue the service. Several close friends and family shared their special memories of my mother. My brother-in-law, Harold Bussell, shared meaningful words from the scripture that Mom would have loved. We concluded the service with Marsha playing the Lord's Prayer. This was a day that truly honored my dear mother.

After the service in San Jose, we traveled to Porterville, CA, where Mom lived and had another memorial service at the Nazarene Church, where she attended. Harold Bussell played the piano this time, Richard offered a prayer, and I did the eulogy. Several of her friends from the church and family members attended this service. It was an honor to be involved in this celebration of life for Mother.

Watch Dog Volunteer

When Mae, our oldest granddaughter, started to attend Women Roberts Elementary School just two blocks from our home, she was in 1st grade. Marsha and I volunteered to help the children in Mae's class with reading. Mrs. Phillips was a wonderful teacher and Mae really liked her. We discovered that children were at different reading levels. Some children like Mae were excellent readers, and we spent less time with them because they could read a book quickly. Since Mae went to bed with books as a little girl, she had an avid desire to learn how to read. However, there were other students who did not have that same desire to read and were very slow readers. Each person was different and we tried to help the individual no matter what level of reading they demonstrated.

As volunteers in 2015, we both had to pay $75 and do a background check with the police department, including fingerprinting. This was a protection for the students, teachers and faculty. This background check was good until Covid in 2020-2022 and then we had to get another background check in order to volunteer to help Sierra's 2nd-grade class with reading. Marsha and I helped with their reading program to encourage the children to become better readers and talk about how important reading is in life. You use it to sing, to use the computer, to text a friend, to cook and many other important functions in life.

I was a Watch Dog volunteer for five years, from 2016-2020, when Covid started. Being a watchdog means that dads, uncles, and granddads volunteer at least one day a year to visit their child's classroom and help out with whatever the teacher needs them to do. Sometimes, it is reading, other times, it involves math, and maybe you get to help with art and physical education with the coach. You are there from 8 am-3:30 pm and discover how stressful teaching can be. Since 40% of the children do not have a father at home, you become a father figure for those children. This is a very rewarding experience, and you will come away with a greater appreciation for teachers. The Watch Dog program is nationally sponsored and provides a higher degree of security with a male volunteer on campus.

Volunteer as a Police Chaplain

After I finally retired as a Presbyterian Minister in 2017, I was asking myself what I wanted to do with my life. I served as a minister for 42 years, and now I have decided to apply to volunteer as a chaplain for the Police Department. I have always appreciated the selfless service many police people put into their work as first responders. They put themselves on the line to protect our community and citizens even when in harm's way. There is a parallel between an Air Force pilot and a policeman in many ways. They both have Type A personalities and are energetic and active in life. Sitting behind a desk is not what they desire; it is an action involving people. They want to be at the center of what is happening rather than being an observer.

As a Type A person, I find myself identifying with these persons, and I especially enjoy being around pilots in the Air Force. They are a unique breed and are fun to be around. Once you earn their respect, they will open up and be your friend. So when I retired, I found myself gravitating towards these men and women who serve their community with a big heart for helping people. I remember that during my first few months working with the police force, I had to "earn the right to be heard" through my words and actions. Police officers are a tight group that keeps to themselves until you build trust with them.

One way I built trust with this community of officers was to spend an 8-hour shift riding along with them in their car. It was important to watch and listen carefully and then ask questions to build a rapport. When you are alone in the car with the officer, there is plenty of time to get to know them and ask personal questions like, "Why did you join the police force?" "What is the hardest part of your job?" "What is your favorite part of your job?" "Do you have a family?" "What is the hardest part of the job for your spouse?" Just taking time to be interested in each person is very important to help break down any walls they might have. As a chaplain, this is the most important thing I could do to see them as real people with tremendous worth. They want to be treated with respect and have someone they can talk with after dealing with difficult situations on the job. They need to be able to release their stress before it negatively builds up in them. This was the privilege I was given when volunteering, often during the night shift.

I was privileged to ride with a former friend of mine who grew up with my oldest daughter, Jewel. They were in the same youth group at First Presbyterian Church in Colorado Springs. I discovered that Ryan Tipley was on the police force and invited me to take rides with him during his night shift. This was a great opportunity for me to catch up with him and his family and enjoy our time together. He was always a real gentleman in helping me find the proper equipment, like a fitting bulletproof vest. He also welcomed me during the officers' briefing at the beginning of their shift. I ended up volunteering for a few years, which was a great experience and gave me a greater appreciation for the men and women in police uniforms.

Hiking With the Guys

After retiring for the 4th time in 2016, I needed a new community of friends to fill the void left by leaving the church. I knew that retirement would bring about a huge adjustment but I did not realize how big the hole would be. It was not only a loss of community but also the lack of purpose that was plaguing me. I believe it is one of the reasons I wanted to apply to the Covenant Presbyterian Church Interim Pastorate position. I felt this would be a good fit because Cathy and Bruce Eschew are members there and Cathy would be on staff part-time with me. Plus, the church is local and I would not have to commute to Pueblo. However, there was one major drawback with this position. I was extremely tired and my body started to fall apart, not knowing that I was suffering from hydrocephalus. Marsha was wise enough to block my application from going through, as she did not want me to fall apart in front of a new congregation. Although I applied and met with the Session, God was gracious enough to keep it from happening.

Never before have I had such a difficult time deciding whether to apply or not. Although Cathy was disappointed with the ultimate outcome, as she was excited to work with me, she understood what was happening with me personally. I knew I needed something to fill the void of community and purpose, and my good friend Don Wallace invited me to join his hiking group of eight guys. We met every Thursday around 9 am and drove 20 miles to higher ground, where we discovered a trailhead. These guys were experienced hikers and had hiking poles and special pants that you could unzip if it got too hot and became shorts. I realized if I was going to be a part of this group, I needed to buy hiking pants, poles and boots.

Most hikes would be 5-8 miles long, and we always climbed a strenuous trail, going from 8,000 feet to 10,000-11,000 feet. These were serious hikers who enjoyed God's beautiful creation and got plenty of good exercise. Most of them attended First Presbyterian Church, where Don taught an Adult Class on Sunday mornings. This was very fitting for Don since his job was being the principal of Cheyenne Mountain Junior High School. Being in education was right up his alley. Don was also a search committee member who hired me as the Minister of Single Adults in 1981. He and his wife, Gail, were nice enough to allow us to stay with their family for a week when we first moved to Colorado Springs until our house was ready.

I enjoyed being around these guys and loved breathing in the fresh air up in the high mountains. It reminded me of going for a hike in the High Sierras with my dad and his friend in search of a pristine lake to fish at. There is something very peaceful about soaking in God's beautiful creation and smelling the fresh pine trees. Most of the time, we enjoy the silence instead of having an ongoing conversation. There were times when one or two of us would get into a profound conversation, but for the most part, it was a time of reflection. Being part of this hiking group was important for me during this huge change in my life.

CrossFit Exercise

One of the things I chose to do after retiring was to join a CrossFit organization. My dentist, Steve Richardson, had joined it several months ago and really enjoyed it. When I had a dentist appointment with him, I talked to him about it and where he attended it. Although there was a CrossFit that was closer to my home, I wanted to be in the same one with Steve for camaraderie. The location I went to was close to Steve's dental office. Steve also encouraged me to join this one because of the leader who was in charge. Although the exercises that you do each day are the same, the personnel are different and can make a large difference in how things are run.

From 2017 to 2019, I became part of this organization for $100 a month. I found it to be a good motivation for me to keep physically healthy. This group not only emphasized the importance of regular physical activity but eating well, too. I signed up for a class from 8:30-9:30 am each morning. My drive to CrossFit was about ten minutes each way. I not only enjoyed the good physical exercise I experienced but also meeting many new people. I especially enjoyed getting to know an ER doctor and his wife who was a physical education teacher in a high school. I also met a police officer who was stationed in Denver, but he lived in Colorado Springs.

Crossfit is a program that emphasizes a balanced program of both cardio and weight training. Each day, a different focus would be used from your arms, legs, chest and balance. It stresses the importance of having a healthy balance of your body. The program would use chin-up bars, dead weights, rope climbing, jogging and the jump rope. They also used a PCV pipe to increase the flexibility of your shoulders and arms as you would move it over your head and behind your back. I remember the first time I tried this I was not able to do this exercise. But as the months went on and my flexibility increased, I was able to complete the full exercise. I still enjoy doing this at home twice a day for flexibility.

When I first started CrossFit, I was not able to do the jump rope exercise either. However, with persistence and practice, my jump roping improved as well. Although I injured my right quad muscle during an annual test by doing too many step up, step down with two 20 lb. weights in my hands, there were many good things that I learned from Crossfit. Overall, it is a good program, but one must be careful not to overdo it. The program is designed to mainly use your body weight as a means of exercise. This part I agree with, but sometimes the use of weights can be detrimental, as happened to me. It did give me a purpose and a time to get out of the house and meet other people. I needed this new discipline during my 4 ½ years when suffering from an unknown disease.

Air Force Academy (AFA) Equestrian

After I retired from being a minister with the Presbyterian Church in July 2016, I was open to doing something entirely different. In 2017, I called Billy Jack, who is the leader of the AFA equestrian organization. Since I am a retired Air Force chaplain and I have an Air Force ID, it is easy to get on the AFA. When I met with Billy Jack, he mentioned to me that Jeanie Springer is in charge of the horse therapy program to help veterans who suffer from PTSD. What was interesting was that Jeanie was a deacon at Faith Presbyterian Church, where I did a one-year internship in 2007. This door just seemed to be a natural fit for me in retirement.

It was a perfect match for me since I worked on a 3000-acre cattle ranch with 1000 head of cattle when I was 16 and 17. One of the things I did while on the ranch was to ride a horse all day once a week when we moved cattle from one windmill area to another. I loved horses, which gave me incredible experience of not being afraid of horses but respecting and working with them. This program taught me to understand and appreciate horses even more than before. They are an amazing animal and very smart.

One of the reasons that they use horses to bring healing to veterans with PTSD is because of their slow heartbeat. In contrast to us humans, who normally have 70-80 heartbeats per minute, the horse's heart beats 40 times each minute. Being next to a horse can automatically help one to calm down and restore their mind and body. My job was to assist a veteran with PTSD to become comfortable with a horse. First, he chose the one that he liked from all the other mares. Normally, the horse that is chosen has a disposition similar to that of the person who chooses the horse. It's amazing how that works.

Next, we would teach them how to groom a horse, which would be very tranquil for both the person and the horse. During this grooming process, it has a strong calming effect on the veteran and they start to become one with the horse. If the person feels comfortable enough, we might also have them clean the four horseshoes of the horse. This kind of exercise builds trust.

The next step is to teach them how to bridle and saddle a horse. This is a building block approach that will lead the individual to eventually ride the horse. Again, the veteran starts to relax around the horse and the horse can feel it. The veteran begins to feel joy and contentment in mastering these steps, and this is evident in his attitude and outlook on life. A major change starts to take place with the individual and they discover healing for their PTSD and begin to sleep better. Others around them also notice a remarkable change in their treatment of people and a general improvement in life. One of the best things about this kind of recovery is it is all-natural. This is very important to people who have seen a psychiatrist and been given prescriptions to help them get better. Most of the time, these veterans are so tired of being put on drugs that often make them feel lethargic and lead to brain fog.

When I worked with horses, I also noticed an improvement in my mental attitude. During this time, I was suffering from hydrocephalus, water on the brain that causes cognitive problems, incontinence, and walking and balance issues. It would often lead me to have brain fog and difficulty with memory. But none of the three neurologists could determine what I had and would only say, "Come back in six months." This was very frustrating for me. I am upbeat and would continue to put my best foot forward but I was suffering. I was also on anti-depressant medication and anti-anxiety pills and struggled to get a good night's sleep. However, being around horses and helping these veterans to get better was rewarding. I had the privilege to be a part of this important horse therapy program for three years until 2020, when Covid invaded us.

Golfing With Friends

Back in 2017, I told Marsha, "If you ever want to learn how to play golf, now is the time. John Plessinger, who was married to Diny Golder, is an excellent golfer and has the patience of job." Marsha was a close friend of Diny so the golfing adventure began as we would meet to play on a small golf course named Cherokee every Saturday morning when the weather was good. Deny was also learning the sport, and it made for a fun foursome. John not only taught us pointers of the golf game but also helped Marsha buy a starter set and added to her clubs as she progressed in the sport. We had more laughs on that course and afterward at lunch.

The price was right at Cherokee, charging only $7/person for the small par three course. This was a perfect course for us to get started in playing this very challenging game. The only thing we had against it was how far we had to travel. It was located in the southeast part of Colorado Springs and would take us 30 minutes to get there. It was much closer to where John and Diny lived.

During these formative years, Marsha and I were not only getting important tips from John but we decided to go ahead and take golf lessons from Golf Tech. Fortunately, they were located up north and only 15 minutes from our home. Since Marsha had never played golf before, she did not have any bad habits that needed correcting. However, I, on the other hand, had played golf when in the Air Force and never had any lessons so I developed all kinds of bad habits. Taking lessons became quite a challenge as I had to undo many bad habits.

Unfortunately, this was during the time I had hydrocephalus and extreme pain in my lower right back and hip. I can remember those were painful years as I could not even stand up for more than a minute without excruciating pain shooting down my right leg. It was very painful to take lessons and practice my golf. But being the positive person I am, I tried to ignore it and try to improve the best I could. I was also struggling with cognitive issues, which did not help my concentration or lack thereof. These were difficult years for me as I pursued learning the game of golf as I thought this would be a great sport for both Marsha and me to enjoy during retirement.

Now fast forward the clock several years and it is now 2022. A lot of history has gone under the bridge, including the sad death of Diny Golder in 2019. Diny fought the good fight and was a real trooper, having gone through numerous surgeries on her back. During this time, she was determined to continue to play golf as she knew how much John enjoyed it. John had incredible patience with Diny, encouraging her and placing her balls down on the course for her to hit. When she got so bad, John would hit both his and her balls off the tee and then Deny would hit short chip shots and put her ball on the green. She had a positive attitude during this time and never complained about any pain she was in. Diny was taking 20-30 pills a day for all her physical problems but was happy to be out of the hospital. Fortunately, Diny had a strong faith in God, and we prayed for her healing. In some ways she was healed and had her life extended many years.

Marsha and I continue to play golf every week with John, weather permitting, as we promised Diny that we would take care of John for her. John misses Diny very much but continues to do well and loves golf. John has played this sport since he was twelve years old. He is a realist, and at times, he will admit, "This is a hard game." He is the owner of Knob Hill Dive Bar in Denver, two blocks from the capital. It is good that he has this job, as it keeps him busy and helps fill the void of Diny's loss.

Wedding Anniversary # 50

Marsha and I wanted to do something special with our family for our 50th Wedding Anniversary. We looked at cruises and a resort stay, but the one that ultimately won was going to a dude ranch for four days. By not flying, we were able to save time and money. Plus, Carlos was not fond of flying with two children under four. We looked into the many dude ranches in Colorado and discovered that most of them were very costly. However, when we were with our dentist, Dr. Steve Richardson, he recommended the dude ranch he has been taking his family to for years. It is not too far away, about four hours, and the cost was very reasonable. We were able to get the whole four day stay for under $4000 for two cabins and eight adults and three children. This included the cost of breakfast and dinner. We brought food for our lunches which worked out well. We invited Harold and Carol Bussell, my sister and husband from California, to join us for this celebration.

We stayed there June 18-22, 2018. Since we were married on June 1, 1968, these dates were perfect for our festive time together. Harold and Carol helped out with raising Sierra for her first three years while the Muros lived in Carpentaria, California. So, it was wonderful to have them help out with babysitting the youngest baby and spend time with Sierra again.

While at Harmel's Ranch Resort next to Gunnison, Colorado, we enjoyed various activities. They had a heated swimming pool and a hot tub. There was a pond that was stocked with rainbow trout that were very hungry. It was easy to cast a line in the lake and catch a fish. This was especially important for the children who loved catching the fish. Most of the fish we tried to release back into the lake. But the children were thrilled with the venture of having a fish caught on your hook and reeling them in. They also had horses ready to ride, so one afternoon, we went on a horseback ride in the forest. It was fun watching the adults having fun trying to control their horses, who were stubborn at times. There was also a recreation room with ping pong and billiards that we used.

Besides the beautiful forest, there was the Taylor River, which ran right through Harmel Ranch and provided excellent opportunities for fishing and white water rafting. On the rafting trip, Mae fell over into the water but was quickly saved. This trip is where Carlos got hooked on fly fishing. He now has his own fly fishing company that he and a colleague created as a part time business. Their company offers fly fishing trips for people to enjoy. Who would have thought that our Wedding Anniversary trip to Harmel Ranch would be the beginning of fly fishing for Carlos? He is completely hooked on this hobby.

There were also miles of hiking trails to enjoy the serene beauty of the mountains. On Thursday night, they had a special barbeque steak dinner with all the country fixings of potato salad, corn on the cob, beans, apple sauce and special cake. This included lemonade or water and hot coffee. Along with this delicious supper were some country western dances to kick up your heels and have fun. This was a wonderful, fun night to remember. There were also Baseball Steaks served on another night for dinner. Everyone in our family had a great time of celebrating life together. Happy 50th Anniversary, Dave and Marsha!

Trip to Disney World and Hilton Head

It was in the fall of 2018, we planned a trip to Disney World with Christian, Jewel and Mae. Our tickets were purchased, and we had bought the 5-day pass for the price of four days. We wanted to make sure we had plenty of time to see the many sights in Disney World. I went through the military plan and saved lots of money. We decided to stay at Shades of Green which is a military property and is half the price of other hotels in the area. It also has a small store to buy food and other items with no tax. The rooms are spacious and quiet. There is also a restaurant on the property with delicious food and a good price. There are buses that pick you up right on the property and go to the various Disney theme parks.

It was a perfect place to stay and get away from the crowds at a comfortable hotel. Once on the bus, it was a 20 minute ride to the theme parks and did not require the expense and hassle of parking. This was an excellent start to the 1st day of Disney World. We ended up visiting all four theme parks: Animal Kingdom, MGM, Magic Kingdom, and the largest one, Epcot, with numerous countries represented. One of the great pluses of Epcot was all the different foods representing the various countries. We enjoyed brats in Germany and cheese fondue in Switzerland. Not to be outdone by the fresh pineapple and ice cream in Hawaii. This was an eater's paradise.

Enjoying the Toy Story ride lets you become a kid again as you play the shooting game from your individual carts to hit the biggest valued targets. What fun to let your hair down and enjoy the game. These games produced great competition among our family members. Just when you thought you were doing well, someone else always beat your score. This was a very humbling event, but it produced lots of laughter and joy as you became a child.

Another favorite of ours was the newest addition to Disney World, a mockup of Star Wars with life-size jets to walk through. There was even a ride that took you on a journey through the galaxy at warp speed with all the fast turns to make it feel real. Disney put a lot of expense, time and work into making this a reality. After a full day at Star Wars, we were tired, and it was time to go back to Shades of Green to eat dinner and relax. This was a smorgasbord, and you could choose any entre. Lots of salad choices, entrees, delicious desserts and drinks. When we were done, we were stuffed and found it hard to move. It was time to take a walk and help digest our food. We decided to go to the small grocery store and see what we could buy before bedtime. As we got to our rooms, we were all tired and ready for sleep.

After enjoying four days in Disney World, it was time to drive to Hilton Head and visit our good friends Doug and Ann Shippy. I've heard of this island but had never been there. This time, we stayed with the Shippys for three days and enjoyed seeing them after many years apart. Ann surprised Marsha with a birthday celebration as we arrived there on Marsha's birthday. It was the perfect way to begin our visit with our friends. Ann is a great cook, so we enjoyed numerous delicious meals with them.

We stayed on the top floor of their spacious, beautiful chalet. It even has an elevator, which took us and our luggage to the 4th floor above the garage. This was a great getaway. Then, they took us on a tour of the island and passed their church, where Ann is a deacon. We also got to see where Ann works part-time at the Disney World resort. This is an ideal job for her to work a few hours a week, earn some spending money, and meet new people. We took them out for lunch and enjoyed sitting by the windows and watching the sailboats. It was so good to enjoy a meal with our special friends and just catch up. The next morning, it was time to say goodbye to Doug and Ann and get on the road again, heading south towards Orlando International Airport.

The rest of the trip was non-eventful except for our visit with Rich and Barbara Walberg, our former neighbors at Norton Air Force Base, whom we hadn't seen in 20 years. It was so fun to have lunch with them and learn about their many adventures. Another reminder to never burn bridges with friends. Rich was a pilot in the Air Force, and Barb, a school teacher. I did some counseling for them to help save their marriage.

Mae and April Fools

I believe that April Fools Day is one of my granddaughter's favorite days of the year. She loves to play jokes on people, and this is a perfect time for her to play her jokes. The first time this happened, she caught me by surprise and totally caught me off guard. By the time I realized it was April 1, the joke was over. She is a sweetheart, and you are not expecting it from her. But Mae does love to tease.

One year, she said that her school was canceled due to bad weather. It was snowing heavily, but it wasn't that bad. By the time we had caught on to her joke school was already in session. Another April fool's joke was when she said her mother was still in her pajamas and could not take her to school. We later found out that she was teasing us, and it was April Fool's Day. Mae was quite good at pulling off April Fool's jokes.

I wonder what she will be doing this year. I'm sure it will be very clever and cute. There is never a dull minute with Mae. We love her very much, and she is a bright spot in our family. We love having her as part of our family. She loves baking cookies with her grandma and snitching cookie dough in the process.

Two Steps Forward and Three Steps Backward

I believe this is how all of us have felt during the COVID-19 pandemic lately. People have been stressed out by being cooped up in their houses and not going anywhere. Too much house rest is not healthy and can cause anxiety and stress within oneself.

Taking two steps forward and three steps backward describes our nation during this pandemic. There have been several problems in our society, like racial tension and police shootings of black people, that have caused tension and division. The January 6th event of hundreds of people storming the capital and breaking into it while Congress was in session was a violent act that caused unbelief and problems. The trial of the police officer in Minneapolis for the death of George Floyd was very unsettling and has left a deep scar on our nation. Plus, the economy and the stock market did poorly, with inflation out of control.

Several vandalism and riots late into the night left our country in a dismal place and have cost cities millions of dollars. This has been going on for over a year with the Black Lives Matter movement after police killed the first African American. This reminds me of the riots and violence in Los Angeles in the 1960s. The National Guard had to be called in to quell the violence. It's amazing how looters and extremists get involved to ramp up the situation. The local folks are not causing the problem. But it is anarchists who are to blame for the insurrection and violence. The local folks are mainly peaceful and don't want any long-lasting destruction.

My Help Comes From God

As I walked outside to mail a letter, I quickly noticed Blodgett Peak and was reminded of the Psalmist's words, "If I lift my eyes up onto the hills, where does my help come from. It comes from my God, the creator of the universe and of us His people." This is the way I often would begin the worship service at Gateway Presbyterian Church which has an incredible view of Pikes Peak. It was a great reminder of who we were worshipping and the reason we came together. It brought God into the service right from the beginning.

In the midst of this Covid pandemic, we need to remember who is ultimately in charge of this world. We can do our best to discover a shot to take to prevent the spread of this horrible pandemic. But this is God's world and His will be done on earth as it is in Heaven. We are just a small blip in the large scheme of things.

Oh Lord, may your will be done in our lives and in your world. We pray not only for the people who live in America and are fighting this pandemic but also for the millions of people in India who are dying daily from this pandemic. Come, Oh Lord, and bring an end to this horrible disease that is causing much suffering on your people. Bring hope where there is despair and light where there is darkness. May this pandemic help turn people to you and cause a revival throughout our world.

May people clearly see that their ultimate hope is only in you, not in medicine or science or government. Thank you for bringing us truth in the midst of confusion. May we turn to your truth, which is lasting and solid and does not change.

I ask for your blessing on Star and Scott's wedding coming up to be a light to all who attend. May people recognize that there is something special happening during the ceremony that is life-changing. Come Holy Spirit, and overshadow the entire ceremony with your presence.

Starlene's Epic Wedding

May 15, 2021

A Destination wedding at Arrowhead Golf Course in Denver, CO, was the event of the year. This was an incredibly beautiful location with tall rock formations in the background, like the Garden of the Gods. You could not have asked for a more stunning setting. On the day of the wedding, it was raining right up to the start of the wedding, and then it miraculously cleared up for the ceremony to begin. Thank you, God for your presence that parted the clouds and brought dryness right at 6 pm when the wedding was scheduled to start. So, all the chairs were brought out again from the tent and dried off for an outdoor ceremony.

The wedding party marched in and took their places up front, waiting for it to start. I had the awesome privilege of walking the bride down into this gorgeous setting as we slowly approached the groom, who was nervously waiting for this moment to begin. As Scott saw the beautiful bride he was overwhelmed with emotion. This was a holy moment and was covered with prayer.

My brother-in-law, Harold Bussell, did the honors of officiating at the beginning and did an excellent job of sharing the historical meaning of the vows. Then he turned the service over to me by asking, "Who gives this woman to be married to this man?" I answered, "Her mother and I do with great joy and love." Then, I was in charge of the service and added humor throughout it when appropriate. I felt very confident and filled with joy as we continued through the ceremony. It was truly a solemn ceremony, but humor brought it to life, and everyone was having a good time. I felt this wedding was bathed in prayer and Jesus was there in a powerful way.

It was a wedding that reflected the joy and happiness of the bride and groom. People had come to witness a sacred moment and were not disappointed. The service was filled with incredible happiness as the bride had waited a long time for this moment. After the ceremony, people moved under the tent as it started to rain again.

A delicious dinner was served, complete with fillet minion, which was tender and tasty. Thanks to Scott and Star, who planned the tasty dinner. Several words were shared by the best man, Tom, and the two maids of honor, Jewel and Chanelle, which continued the levity.

After these words were shared, it was time to break open the dance floor, and lots of people danced. Starting with the bride and groom and a surprise dance with Star and her father. Things broke loose and all had fun. Most people were no longer seated but were on the dance floor, kicking loose with their moves. The DJ did not have to encourage people to dance; it was just happening. The day ended as it began with great joy and celebration.

Thank you, Star, for all the work you and Scott put into organizing this epic event. It had your fingerprints all over it. What a beautiful celebration for two special people. This will go down as one of the greatest celebrations in our lives story. You spent our money well and wisely. We love you, Star and Scott. Your wedding more that exceeded our expectations.

Surprise House Flood
In the Kitchen

It was a crazy inadvertent accident that happened on Saturday, July 10, 2021, before cutting the grass. Marsha was leaving to get her hair cut and I added more water in the sink on top of the frozen turkey to help it defrost. Unfortunately, I left the water going on the turkey and went outside to cut the grass. Completely forgetting about the running water, I was engrossed in getting the lawn cut and edged before Marsha returned home. When she returned home one hour later, she was very surprised to discover a flooded kitchen floor that had gone under the cupboards and into the dining room carpet.

I felt stupid but couldn't cry over spilt milk, but needed to help her soak up the flood with bath towels. This was the very day that Mark and Bob Garcia were going to be staying with us for a few days. I felt horrible for making a careless mistake. Marsha got on the phone with USAA home insurance to discover that we were covered except for a $1000 deductible. This saved us thousands of dollars.

First, the mitigation people showed up that night at 8 pm and started to put their resources in the kitchen and down in the basement. There were lots of fans and equipment to suck up the moisture in the floors and air. It was very loud and was like a jungle gym with all their booby traps and hoses. Mark said it reminded him of being in a noisy airport. The temperature got up in the 80s, so we ate breakfast outside in the backyard, which was very nice.

This noise and inconvenience went on for five days to dry out the wood, walls and ceiling. It reminded me of when we had our carpet replaced, and the many days we were out of sorts.

Finally, they came by on July 15 with the good news that the floor and basement were dry enough to remove their equipment, and we finally had a semblance of quiet return on the main floor. It's amazing how you get used to the loud noise and just put up with it. It was sure nice to have the quiet return and the lack of workmen tramping through our home.

The final plan is to get the mitigation finished by July 17 so the restoration can begin their work. We leave for Mayo Clinic in Phoenix the same day so we are also in the process of packing for our trip. We are flying on Southwest Airlines from Colorado Springs to Phoenix, a direct flight, which will be nice. I am hoping and praying for some positive tests and appointments at Mayo Clinic to overcome my brain issue.

Mayo Hospital Visit

Dr. Adam Robinson got me into the Mayo Clinic to check out my hydrocephalus. Marsha and I flew from Colorado Springs to Phoenix on Southwest Airlines, a 1 ½ hour flight on July 17, 2021. We had an excellent flight and then took the shuttle to the rental car lot, where we rented a car from Budget. It was a new Toyota Camry, so Marsha felt very comfortable driving it. The Camry was similar in size and feel to our Toyota Avalon. Marsha did all the driving and did an excellent job.

Marsha brought her GPS and found our hotel, Sleep Inn, with no problems. Normally, I would do all the driving, picking up our rental car and checking into the hotel. She confessed to me that she did not realize how much I did behind the scenes. She did a great job getting everything done, including checking me in online.

Our stay at Sleep Inn was very good for the price. It was very quiet, and they had us pick up our breakfast in a bag at the front counter. We had our choice between small waffles or a bean burrito to be warmed up in the microwave. I believe Marsha and I were the only long-term guests, as it was very empty. They had a small health club in one of the rooms with two treadmills, an elliptical machine, free weights and fresh water.

The hotel also had a small pool 30' x 12', from 3' to 5'. It was perfect for doing laps and swimming in it. Because it was over 100 degrees outside, the pool was perfect for swimming. I enjoyed using my goggles and did several laps before going to the hospital.

Our hotel was only three miles away from Mayo Clinic so it was perfect for Marsha to drive from each morning and return to at night. She also felt very safe there and could sleep well.

On the day we arrived in Phoenix, we decided to visit the Aquarian. It was a good experience to visit the many fishes and mammals. Marsha took many pictures and shared them with the family.

The next day was another day off after getting my covid check-up, which was done outside in the parking lot. A nurse came up to the car and used a long stick to put up my right nostril and get a sample. Fortunately, it came back negative. Then I went and got my blood done at the Mayo Clinic and had three vials removed. Everything was normal, and I was admitted for my 48-hour spinal tap from my back. I guess it was considered a surgery and very serious. I had to stay in the hospital for three days and two nights. Everything went very well for the drain, and no negative effects until after being discharged. Then, I had severe headaches and could not keep my head up. I also had stomach sickness and emptied my stomach violently four times. But afterward, my headache lessened, and I could get up and move around.

I forgot to mention that on the second day in Phoenix, we decided to visit the Musical Instruments Museum and found it to be fascinating. There were hundreds of instruments from every country in the world. We had a special listening device that allowed us to hear music from all kinds of people. We spent four hours walking through this museum and really enjoyed it. What a great way to spend our free time in Phoenix.

Marsha's Paintings

A star was born when Marsha started doing the painting of many pictures. She loves to paint and is quite good at it. Talk about a variety of pictures, everything from people to flowers to trucks. She is very talented in her realistic paintings. Marsha loves to copy things and is very precise in her efforts. Realism is her strength in painting. Her dad would often say to her, "Oh, Marsha, your mother would be so proud of you." This was his way of saying, "You did a great job in an area in which your mother was involved." It was also his way of congratulating her for a job well done.

When the art gallery she was a part of closed last summer, she had several pictures to bring home. We ended up with numerous excellent paintings to put up in our home. They ended up being placed along the stairwell, which really looked good. When friends came over to say hello, we invited them to our home, and they saw all of Marsha's paintings. They often would ask how much the paintings were and then offered to buy one. This became our new business. She also started getting commissioned to paint new items from friends and colleagues. This was a high compliment to her and kept her busy with her painting.

Congratulations, Marsha, on a job well done!!! You have an excellent gift! I LOVE YOU!!!

Year of Surgeries

It all started with my brain surgery for hydrocephalus on September 20, 2021. I am so glad I went through with it although the doctors were not promising me any good results. I felt like I had come to the end of my rope, and there was nowhere else to go but having the surgery. The doctors told me that if they saw any improvement in my walking, that would be all they could expect. Dr. Turkmani said they usually could expect only one improvement in better walking but not in balance, cognition or stopping the incontinence. When I told him I had experienced improvement in all four areas, he said that was unheard of and credited the power of prayer as the key. He said. "You had a miracle."

Evidently, the rest of my family did not want me to get all the attention. So Jewel had a hysterectomy surgery in January and is doing amazingly well four weeks later. The extreme pain in her neck is now gone; thank you, Lord. The physical therapist believes it was caused by how they had her head positioned during surgery on her back. He said, Jewel, your neck is like you were in an automobile accident and had a severe whiplash. As a result, she not only had extreme pain but was nauseated for several days after surgery. She is doing much better now and left her home for the first time last Friday to celebrate Carlos' birthday. It has been a slow but good recovery from her surgery.

Not to be outdone, Chanelle tore her Achilles tendon when playing volleyball at Scott's gym with the family the day after Christmas. After going to the doctor and getting an MRI, the doctor said she needed to have surgery to repair the damage. Chanelle was glad to learn from the doctor that her tear was not as bad as he first thought. She is now in a cast and has to use crutches and a scooter to keep all the weight off her right ankle while it heals for six weeks. Unfortunately, she tore her right foot, so she cannot drive. I have been appointed the head chauffeur to take her to the doctors, etc. She is doing quite well with her handicap.

Starlene did not want to be left out and is looking at having surgery on her left foot from a bad tear that happened many years ago in high school when playing soccer for the Air Force Academy cadets. Her ankle never fully healed and she reinjured it when playing volleyball a few weeks ago. She is waiting to see what the specialist says after getting an MRI. She may need to have surgery; just not sure yet.

Marsha, mama bear, wants to be included in this party of surgeries and will be having a rotator cuff surgery in three days on February 2, 2022. We borrowed a cold therapy device to help manage her pain and keep the swelling down. She has been cooking up a storm to have a lot of food choices that were put in the freezer. Everything from soups to chili beans has blessed our meals. I guess she doesn't want hot dogs and pizza for all the meals. We are in excellent hands and ready for her surgery. Thank you, Marsha, for your gourmet cooking and excellent preparation.

Phoenix Zoo

On September 29, 2021, nine days after my brain surgery, we visited the Phoenix Zoo. It was a great way to stretch our legs, walk for four hours, and test out my balance after my surgery. I was surprised at how good I felt and was able to keep up with Marsha. Fortunately, it was not too hot, and for the most part, it was fairly flat.

We had a good time walking the 110 acres that housed various animals and reptiles. We enjoyed seeing all the animals and watching them play with one another. They even had these large animal scooters you could rent and ride around on them. Someone had a clever idea and it was working.

The only disappointment was the giraffes were too far away to enjoy and the bears were sleeping in this heat. The crowd was small, which made it nice to walk around. I did a leisure stroll and found I could walk again without any pain from my right hip and lower back. It felt so good to be pain-free and keep up with my wife. Hopefully, this will stay with me, and I will remain pain-free from my lower right back and hip. The MRI showed I have L3-L6 and S1 tightness of the vertebrae, which was causing my pain. After my surgery, I was pain-free. Dr. Turkmani says it is probably from my three weeks of inactivity. I still think God touched my lower back and hip to bring healing to those areas as a bonus. We will find out when I am able to go back to golf after six weeks from the surgery. I am praying for a pain free miracle of my L3-6 and S1 which would be wonderful so I can start golfing again. Thank you, Lord.

Brain Surgery

September 20, 2021

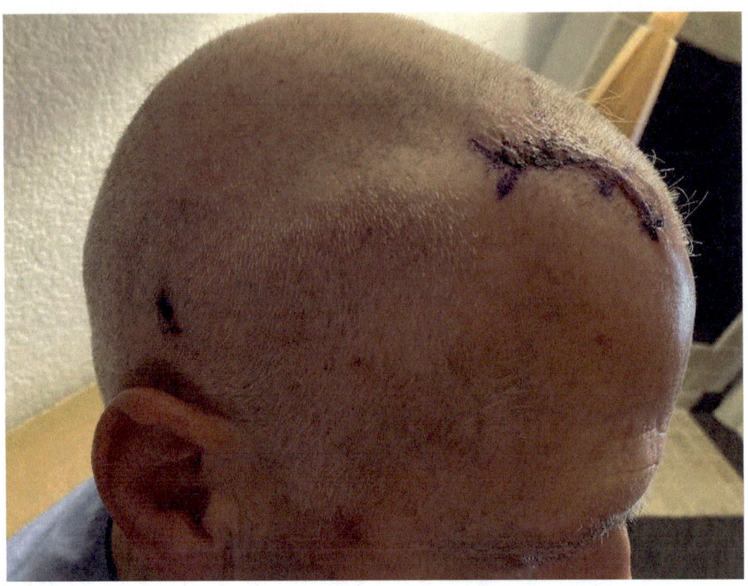

Fortunately, my brain surgery was scheduled for 8:00 am at Mayo Clinic in Phoenix. I got up at 6:00 am and took another shower to make sure my whole body was very clean, including my scalp. They request two showers before the surgery—one the night before and one the morning of the surgery. They would go over the key areas with alcohol to make it very sterol.

I had to fast eight hours before surgery and had nothing to drink two hours prior to the surgery. I was allowed only clear drinks six hours before the surgery. They wanted to make sure I would not get sick during and after the surgery.

I checked into the hospital through the main door and answered all the questions that I did not have Covid. The

COVID-19 pandemic started in January 2020 and was a global epidemic, killing thousands of people throughout the world. Three different vaccines had been created to combat Covid. Unfortunately, some people refused to get vaccinated and suffered the consequences.

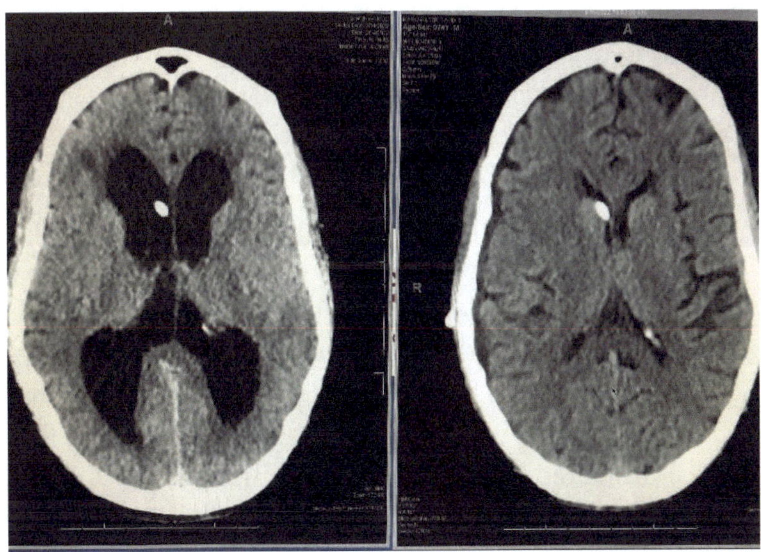

Then a nurse took me into a private room, took all of my vital signs (temperature, blood pressure, weight and height) and handed me a hospital garb to change into. Another nurse stuck me with a needle and hooked me up with two IVs, one in the left arm for fluid during the operation and afterward and one in the right wrist in case they needed a blood transfusion. I was also strapped with a blood pressure cup to monitor my blood pressure continuously.

According to my wife the surgery only took 90 minutes with three doctors in charge. There was the neurosurgeon, the antiseptic doctor, and a general surgeon. Plus there were several nurses to assist with whatever needed to be done. I had a deep peace through this whole process, thanks to all the prayers that were being offered for me. I quickly fell asleep and did not feel a thing until it was over.

When I woke up, I was in the recovery room with ten other patients who were recovering from surgery. With that many patients, there was always someone who was in extreme pain and crying out to the nurse for help. I was monitored by a nurse who was to make sure all was well. When she had to leave her station, another nurse quickly took her place. They were continually monitoring my pain and giving me pain medicines to help. I mainly took Tylenol with iodine to supplement it.

I was surprised that I had to remain in the recovery room for 6-7 hours, waiting for a permanent room to open up. This was mainly due to Covid. Mayo Clinic in Phoenix is building another unit to add 100 new rooms, which are definitely needed. When I finally reached my own private room, Marsha was able to join me and was glad to see me. She told me that Dr. Turkmani told her that the operation went very well. I met the nurse who would be with me until 7:00 pm. They work a 12-hour shift, and soon I would meet the nurse who would be taking care of me all night long. They were very professional and supported me. They even put in my order for meals. I found the food to be very tasty with a large selection to choose from the menu.

That night, I was awake a lot due to my heart monitor going off from a low heartbeat and other issues. I was totally surprised when I got up to use the restroom that my balance had vastly improved. Praise God. Before being discharged from the hospital, I needed to see the PT therapist, who put me through many walking and balancing tests and cognitive tests, too. By 11:00 am, I was dismissed and driving to our Residence Inn at Marriot. I was exhausted and took a 3-hour nap, which felt wonderful.

Movie Date

On September 27, Marsha and I went to watch the movie "Respect" with Aretha Franklin in a small theater in Scottsdale. The theater had only two rows with a total of 12 seats. They were recliners and very comfortable. There was even a waitress who took our food order and served us. Only 12 seats were in this theater, which was phenomenal. We enjoyed eating a large popcorn order of half Carmel corn and half regular. It reminded me of being in Jewel and Christian's theater at their home.

The movie "Respect" was a story about Aretha Franklin's life. Very sad and moving as we witnessed the home she was raised in with a strict father and grandfather. Her mother and father did not have a good marriage as he was very cruel to her. It is amazing that she stayed with him for as long as she did. The song "Respect" spells out what Aretha wanted for her mother and herself. She lived a very tragic life that had many down moments that came from her childhood background.

In spite of the movie, Marsha and I had a good time watching a flick in a small setting. There were only three other people in the whole theater. I liked seeing the movie "Ford vs Ferrari" much more, showing the true Ferrari spirit and encouraged me to visit the Ferrari dealership in Scottsdale. We enjoyed seeing these beautiful cars that ran from $350000 to one million. A bit out of our price tag, but the salesman was good, saying it is an investment as the price will be much higher when you sell it years later. It was fun to see several Ferraris and to walk through Penske Museum where several race car winners of the Indianapolis were there. It was fun to get out of the motel room and stretch my legs.

Visit and dinner at Carrabbas

One of the joys of our trip to Phoenix for brain surgery at Mayo Clinic was discovering the contentment of eating out at Carrabbas, which was walking distance from the Marriot Residence Inn, where we stayed for 17 nights. The first time we ate there, we met this wonderful young waitress named Rachael. She was absolutely superb in her service and efficiency. She was very sweet with excellent serving manners. All three times we ate there, we gave her a large tip. Even when we went and had drinks at the bar before leaving, we surprised her with a $20 tip.

Marsha and I decided to split a Parisian dinner with an extra salad for dinner. That was plenty for the two of us at night. Kenny Nolan and his wife, Ann, and daughter, Kendra, lived only 30 minutes away. Kenny was the custodian at First Presbyterian Church in Pueblo, where I served as an Interim Pastor for nine months after I retired from Gateway Presbyterian Church in 2015. Kenny was an excellent custodian and very friendly and welcoming to us every Sunday when we arrived. We invited them to join us for dinner as our guests at no other restaurant than Carrabbas. They were very pleased with the choice of the restaurant as they hadn't eaten there for a long time. Another great meal was enjoyed by all, and of course, Rachael was our waitress. It was a nice surprise to reconnect with Kenny and his family.

Ride Home from Phoenix

October 1-2, 2021

We drove home from Phoenix in our in our 2017 Honda CRV on October 1 and drove to Gallup, NM, to stay overnight. The Honda got 33 mpg on this trip, which is very good for a non-hybrid auto and large vehicle, especially in light of Marsha and Star driving 80-85 on the freeway, where the speed limit was 75. We decided to fill up with gas once the gas gauge was half full, unlike what we did on the drive out there, almost running out of gas twice.

We had the car packed full with all our suitcases and supporting items. It was amazing how good gas mileage we got with our entire luggage and traveling that fast. Fortunately, there were no tickets and no accidents or flat tires. I decided to read "Healing Depression for Life" and finished the whole book on this two-day marathon. When I found some material I wanted to share with them, I read it out loud. To my surprise, I was able to read it with speed and excellent comprehension. I hadn't had that ability for several years, and this was another part of my healing from the brain surgery.

The second day, we got up after sleeping well and started the second half of the trip. Originally, we were only going to drive to Raton NM, but Marsha and Star were feeling good, and it was only another 2 1/2 hours more, so we drove all the way home to sleep in our own beds. This was the right decision as we got home around 7:30 pm instead of the next day.

We unpacked the car and moved back into our home, which felt so good. Plus, the next day, we had plans to have everyone over for lunch and bought a bucket of Kentucky

Fried Chicken with rolls, Coleslaw and beans. This was a great way to celebrate our reunion with our family. I shared about God's miracle of healing my brain and improvement in all four areas: walking, balance, incontinence gone, and improved cognition. Dr. Turkmani said that normally there is an improvement in one area (walking) but never in all four areas. This was definitely God's hand upon me during this surgery. Praise God!!

Suffering for Five Years

After my brain surgery, I was now able to walk faster and keep up with Marsha, which she liked. I used to be able to run circles around her but not anymore. She loved I was more talkative and vocal and even spoke louder. She loved that the brain fog was gone, and I was present with her once again. She loved I was able to help out around the house with many projects. Right after getting out of the surgery, she told me, "I really missed you. It is so nice to have you back as my new husband." Our love life has returned, and we are more affectionate again. Praise God for the healing of better balance and walking, no more incontinence, and improved cognitive including my memory.

When Star, Christian and I went snow skiing for our annual ski trip at Christmas time, I fell numerous times. I usually would fall down 1-2 times a day. What was worse, I could not figure out how to put my skis back on. Star then insisted that I see my doctor and request to be checked out for Parkinson's disease and see a neurologist. For the next five years, I was suffering, trying my best to figure out what was wrong. I made appointments with three different neurologists in Colorado Springs and Denver at Anschutz, a research hospital, and they would say, "We don't know what you have, but we will see you in six months." I got so tired of hearing this without any definite cure. During this time, they ruled out Parkinson's disease, dementia, Louie body disease and other mental diseases, but still no answer.

Finally, Dr. Adam Robinson, a good Christian physician and my primary care doctor said, "Dave, you have suffered long enough. I will try to get you into Mayo Clinic in Phoenix and have them treat you." Even the neurologist and neurosurgeon were not sure at first what I had. They thought it might be hydrocephalus, but not 100% positive. So they ran all kinds of tests on me, including an MRI, CAT scan, blood tests, and many more. I even had a 48-hour spinal drain test on my back that would better rule out hydrocephalus. This test would assimilate what a shunt would do by inserting a needle in the lower back to drain the ventricle in the brain with too much water. Even after taking this test it wasn't crystal clear if I had it or not. Through a PT test there seemed to be a slight improvement in my walking. They said I might have it but weren't positive, but if we wanted to get a shunt installed in my brain to help clear the excessive water they would do it. We felt like we had come to the end of our rope with no other hope, so we did it.

Blue Rubber Bracelet

After my brain surgery on September 20, 2021, Sarah Clark visited me at home. Sarah had been through two brain shunt surgeries, one when a child and the second one as an adult. Having been through these surgeries has made her a real encourager to anyone like me who just had the surgery. Sarah was a teacher for the nursery school at the Air Force Academy for several years, but recently switched jobs and works at "Build a Bear" in Colorado Springs. When she visited me, she brought me a white bear I call cuddles that simulate having a brain shunt put in his brain. From the brain, it has a wire tube that goes behind an ear, down the neck and chest and ending in the stomach. This is a reproduction of what I had done to me to get the excessive fluids off my brain and drain it into my abdomen. This is really a complex surgery when you look at all the variable parts that have to function properly.

Besides the "Build a bear" gift, Sarah gave me a Blue Rubber Bracelet with the initials "No more BS." I wear the bracelet 24 hours a day, reminding me of the incredible brain surgery that was performed on me on September 20, 2021. It's amazing with the miracle of modern medicine, what these skilled neurosurgeons are able to accomplish. I always wanted to be more holy, so drilling a hole in my skull to place the shunt to remove the excessive water on my brain is right on target. The Blue Rubber Bracelet that I wear around the clock and says, "No more BS," stands for the slogan "no more brain surgery." The goal of the hydrocephalus organization is to find a cure to avoid brain surgery. This is such a common surgery, especially among babies and young children. As their bodies and head grow, a second operation is usually necessary to correct the growth. This is why Pediatricians measure the baby's head when they are born.

I wear this bracelet as a constant reminder of the ultimate healing that happened to me from that surgery. Although, the brilliant neurosurgeon, Dr. Turkmani, warned me before the surgery that brain surgery is dangerous and there is often a lack of good results. He said, "If we get any improvement, it will most likely be improvement in your walking only." He went on and said, "But often, there is no improvement at all." So much for encouragement from one of the best doctors at Mayo Clinic. But when I told Dr. Turkmani after the surgery, "Thank you, thank you, thank you for being God's Hands and healing me. I've got my life back. I'm a new person." I told him I had improvement in all four areas: walking, balance, no more incontinence, and cognitive focus. He quickly added, "I can't take credit for that." Marsha added, "Doctor, we had an army of prayer warriors praying for David." He said, "That was the key. A miracle has occurred." This little blue bracelet reminds of this fact and to be grateful every day for this miracle.

Moab Trip

Nov 4-7, 2021

This was our first trip of seven trips planned for this year ahead. Now that I'm so much better from the brain surgery, it is time to celebrate life and enjoy God's creation and each other through traveling. It is so good to feel good again and enjoy life. God is so good. Thank you, God, for the miracle of a new life. May we be ever grateful for all you have given us.

We left on Thursday after Marsha's hair cut at 10:30 am. We drove in the Avalon for 400 miles, reached our destination, and stayed in the Quality Inn in Moab. The summer crowds were gone and there were few people on the road and staying at the hotel. Our big surprise was how filthy the bathroom floor was when Marsha mopped it up with a towel. The staffing was minimal because of Covid and workers refusing to work for minimum wages. With all the free money that the government has given away people are feeling entitled and don't want to work.

We averaged 49 mpg in our Avalon, which is a hybrid. Still not as good as an electric car, but less expensive to purchase. The first day after travel we ate breakfast at the hotel and then took a ride to see Arches National Park. When we passed through the entrance, we were finally able to use our National Park Pass that we purchased years ago and it was free. It was nice to make use of something from the past.

We witnessed many beautiful arches and spectacular red rocks with the La Salle Mountains in the backdrop, christened with white snow peaks. They are part of the Rockies mountain range.

The second day, we went to "Dead Horse Point" and witnessed an incredible view of the Colorado River (Green River) winding around the canyons that were 2000 feet below. This was breath taking. Legend has it that the cowboys rounded up mustangs and led them to the Point and used the cliff and branches as a corral. They would choose the ones they wanted to ride and leave the other ones there locked in to die of dehydration.

We did a lot of hiking on the rocks and followed the trail around the rim of the canyon.

Another place we briefly visited was Canyonlands, which was quite different from anything we had seen. We stopped at their visitor center and had our picnic lunch on their patio. They had an old hand pump to get water in this desert land with a sign to please use sparingly. We went shopping in the store and bought a few souvenirs.

Happy Thanksgiving Chuck

Looking backward, we have a lot to be grateful for. First, thinking of the many wonderful Thanksgivings we celebrated with the Keith's in Los Angeles is amazing. This was Uncle Chuck's favorite holiday, and he cooked up a storm with the Turkey and all the fixings to go along with it. I remember he had two portable ovens in the garage going and then a huge amount of food he was cooking in their kitchen. There was always plenty to eat, and he would put a positive spin on it as a teacher to make sure the children knew why we're celebrating Thanksgiving. It was much more than just time off of work to gather with the family and friends and say "Thank you."

It was foundational to our nation in giving thanks for what we have. It was also a time to share our blessings with others who are less fortunate. We are blessed to be a blessing. This is something in the Bible that sounds loud and clear. We are not blessed to hoard our blessings but to give them away. Thank you, God!!! This would be a better place to live if people would remember and practice this. We have been given much to give away.

One thing about Uncle Chuck, he was very generous to the T. Whether it was putting little packages in our motor home to enjoy on our trip or taking us to their swimming pool, there was a spirit of giving that overshadowed him. We were blessed to have an Uncle Chuck in our life. We see the same trait in his wife and children, so the legacy goes on. He enjoyed life to the fullest and even turned life into moments of humor. His motto was, "Live Well, Laugh Often, Love Much."

Practicing Guitar

I got up this morning ready to go and practice my guitar. It is Advent, so I switched over to Christmas music, which I love. Today, I plan to practice the guitar since it has been several weeks since I made music. My plan is to toughen up my fingertips which are very sensitive in playing a steel string guitar. I am having trouble hitting the right keys in my typing. This is such good practice to get back into writing my memoir. Thank you for your encouragement and help in this goal.

I love playing the guitar as it is very peaceful to sing along with it. This morning it felt good to play some of the Christmas tunes and sing them. It has been a full year since playing them.

It helps bring in the Christmas spirit and I look forward to celebrating Christmas. It is so much fun watching Brooklyn be a child and play her games. She is so spirited in whatever she does, you cannot help but love her. Whether she is singing or dancing, she is very infectious in her actions. It is fun being "Paka" at Christmas time.

Watching the "The Chosen"

This movie was recommended for me to watch from several people whom I trust. So Marsha and I started watching it recently and we have found it to be well done and follow the truth in the Bible. We finished the first series already and are ready to begin part 2. It is the best Christian movie series we have seen in a long time. The acting is superb, and it follows the Bible account of Jesus and his disciples very closely. The actors are excellent and we are hooked at watching this series.

We love the drama and are very grateful for no advertisements. It is easy to understand, and have found it to be very realistic regarding the characters and how they are portrayed. The series gives a very realistic twist to the background and the character development of Jesus and his closest followers. We have already seen the first eight episodes in just the last three days. Once you start watching it, you don't want it to quit. Even the character of Jesus is very realistic and not overdone.

I love the many different settings the movie develops, which are probably how it actually happened. For example, doubting Thomas is seen as a provider of the wine at the bridal party dinner in Cana of Galilee. His personality would ultimately fit into "doubting Thomas." Always worrying about the banquet and making sure there was enough wine. It would be very embarrassing for the bridal party if they ran out of wine. This was his personality when he doubted the other disciples that Jesus was really alive after his death. He would not believe the disciples had seen the risen Lord. He said, "Unless I see his face and feel the marks of where the nails went into his skin, I will not believe." He was a true pragmatist and did not want to be fooled. So Jesus tells him to come and feel the places where they put the nails in my wrist.

"The Chosen" is one television series we are glad we discovered. Watching it encouraged us in our faith and we are looking forward to seeing the rest of the segments.

Marsha's Rotator Cuff Surgery

I took Marsha into surgery on February 2, 2022, at 6 am to the surgery center at Research and Chapel Hills, where Dr. Kobioshi performed a rotator cuff procedure. That morning it was only eight degrees, and there was 8" of snow on the road, so we left plenty of time to make the trip. Fortunately, there were very few cars on the road due to the snowstorm, which was ice patches and a frozen tundra. But when we got there, they were ready for Marsha, and everything went smoothly.

I talked with the doctor after the surgery, and he was very pleased with the way everything went for her right shoulder. He said there was a major tear and it needed to be fixed, but the prognosis was very good for her future recovery. This was very good news as she had been suffering from it for several months. He was a nice doctor and shared with me only a positive outcome. Marsha really liked him as a physician and person.

The first night after the surgery was difficult as she had trouble sleeping because her throat kept on fighting congestion from the surgery. The second night wasn't much better, but she finally got a good 3-hour nap the following day. This really helped. Then, on the 3rd night, she was having a hard time breathing, and I could hear her wheezing a lot.

Thank you, Karen Thompson, our neighbor, for bringing over a large lasagna dish enough for the Muro family, too. Then I received a telephone call from Vicky Monaque, volunteering to bring dinner for next Monday night. She plans to cook either meatloaf or ham for dinner, enough for the Muros, too. What fabulous neighbors we have and Karen and

Ed Hunt called last night to check to see how Marsha was doing. Thank you, Lord, for such great neighbors.

Marsha seems to be doing good with very little pain and is taking Ibuprofen and Tylenol to manage any pain. We are blessed not to have to take any strong pain killers for her shoulder. We are using the cold ice machine to help manage the pain and swelling. It seems to really help with her shoulder pain. Thank you, Ed Hunt for allowing us to borrow your cold ice machine and Joyce Peluso also. Mike Gebhardt was also a blessing in giving us clear instructions on what helped him with both his surgeries.

Shocking Setback

On February 6, 2022, I experienced a horrible change in my hydrocephalus. I had my shunt installed in my brain to correct my hydrocephalus (water on the brain) on September 20, 2021, and experienced a miracle that improved all four areas. Before the surgery at Mayo Clinic in Phoenix, AZ, I struggled with my cognitive (lights were out, and memory was poor), my walking was slow, I shuffled, and balance wasn't stable, and I had incontinence problems. After the surgery performed by neurosurgeon Dr. Turkmani, I improved in all four areas dramatically. I told Dr. Turkmani, "Thank you for being God's hand in healing me and giving my life back. I improved in all four areas." Dr. Turkmani couldn't believe it as they usually only get a little improvement in one area. Marsha told him, "We had an army of prayer warriors praying for David." He said with a smile, "That was the key."

After enjoying a new life for 4 ½ months, on February 5, I suddenly reverted back to the way I was before the surgery. This was a frightening event for both Marsha and me. What happened that changed? So Marsha started the process to see Dr. McVickers, the neurosurgeon, here in Colorado Springs. He needed two tests before an appointment, and he was out of the office, so Marsha called Dr. Turkmani, and he ordered a CT brain scan and a DX, which is an x-ray from the top of my head to the bottom of my stomach, to see what was going on. I went to a local imaging office to get these procedures done on February 14, 2022, and they showed that my ventricles in my brain had enlarged with water. Dr. Turkmani recommended that we have a neurosurgeon in Colorado Springs change the shunt setting from 2 to 1.5, which will increase the amount of fluid being drained from my brain to my abdomen.

When Marsha called our local neurosurgeon, Dr. McVickers, to get an appointment to adjust the setting, he was out of the office, and the earliest opening for me to see him would be March 17, more than a month away. I was put on a waiting list for any cancellations. A God thing happened and they called that afternoon and said there was a cancellation and Dr. McVickers could see me on February 24, the day after he returned. Praise God!

On February 24, Marsha, Jewel and I went to see Dr. McVickers. We had met him in April 2018 when he said, "You're an excellent candidate for a shunt surgery. When do you want to do it?" However, we requested he do a few more tests, like a spinal tap and a cognitive test. After looking at the test results, he said, "I'm sorry. The pressure wasn't what he expected, and doing surgery wouldn't make any difference." So when we met him this time, he apologized, "Sorry I missed it" and said he was obviously wrong and blew it. Doctors are human, and he made the best decision because brain surgery is dangerous.

We did not hold that against him, although it would have been nice to have had the surgery three years earlier as I was suffering a lot and not getting any help from my three neurologists. I was very frustrated when I would see them, and they would say, "We aren't sure what you have. Come back in six months." There are only so many times you can hear this before discouragement sets in. Finally, my primary care doctor, Dr. Adam Robinson, said, "Dave, you have suffered long enough. Let me see if I can get you into Mayo Clinic in Phoenix." I felt like I was in a dark wilderness shortly after I retired in July 2016. I lived with these horrible symptoms for five long years.

This whole experience was a real "God Thing." God is good all the time, and His plan and timing for me was right. During my wilderness experience, I was given medicine for Parkinson's Disease, due to my shuffling, but it made no difference, so Parkinson's was ruled out. Louie Body disease was also ruled out. Even when I went to the Mayo Clinic in May 2021, the head neurologist did not think I had hydrocephalus. He sent me to the Neurosurgeon, so we came back to the Mayo Clinic in July to take a 48-hour Lombard spinal drain, which would simulate what a shunt would do in my brain. Even with this test they were still not sure a brain surgery would work but said they saw a slight improvement from that test in my walking. Marsha did not see it. We were literally at the end of my rope, and after talking with the girls, we decided to go ahead with the surgery. Thank God I did, as my life has improved dramatically. I give God all the glory and praise for my miraculous healing and for being with me during the dark time in the wilderness. For five years, I kept a positive attitude the best I could and followed Grandma Jean Rech's advice when she told me, "David, sometimes when life is difficult, you just have to fake it until you make it." Thank you, Jean, for that wise counsel.

Trip to Branson MO

One of my bucket lists was to take a road trip to visit Branson and take in the shows there. Branson is a small town of 10,000 people built on several hills. It is kind of a mini Christian Las Vegas with a strip that has one theater after the next. I understand during the summer it is bumper-to-bumper traffic. Fortunately, we went there on April 5-10, 2002, so the traffic and restaurants were light.

We saw the show "Jesus" with three other couples at the Sight and Sound Theater. It was a fabulous production with a 150-foot stage, and the theater had seats for 2,000 people. There are over 1200 LED light panels behind the stage, video production to make it seem real, along with huge moving sets that were incredible. We had the privilege of seeing it with Don and Nancy Ummel, Mike and Willie Munson, and Dick and Pat from Florida. The first two couples are from Bell Vista, Arkansas, so they only had to drive two hours to meet us there.

Don and Nancy were members at Gateway Presbyterian Church when I was the pastor there. They came in 2009 and then left to move to Arkansas in 2012 to be closer to her family. We had not seen them since then. So, it was fun reconnecting and sharing many delicious meals together. One of the lunches, there was a live singer who was quite good and sang a wide range of music.

The hardest part of the trip was the drive on I70, fighting cross and headwinds as we drove across Kansas and tornado alley. The wind was blowing so hard it was white-knuckle driving.

Lots of gusts of winds up to 60 mph. Many of the large 18-wheel trucks were having quite a challenge keeping their truck on the road. Our 2020 Avalon, which sits very low to the ground and is aeronautically designed, did quite well in spite of the winds. But our gas mileage was much lower than normal. No fun in driving in this kind of weather, but at least it wasn't snowing or raining. When we stopped at the rest areas, it was so cold and windy that we couldn't even go for a walk.

Incredible Trip to Canada

One of my bucket lists is to enjoy the Rocky Mountaineer train ride through the Canadian Rockies. Marsha and I finally did it on April 22-May 3, 2022. After God healed me on Sept 20, 2021, from my hydrocephalus (water on the brain), I was able to walk, and my balance was back; no more incontinence, my memory improved and brain fog was gone. It was an absolute miracle. I had my life back, and I was a new person. I told Marsha we were going to travel and enjoy life together. I have wanted to do this trip for ten years as people would tell me you have to do it.

So we got our flight to Vancouver, BC, arranged and proved we had all our covid shots, including two boosters, so we could enter Canada. We had to fill out numerous information on our cell phones on a website called "Arrive Canada." Poor Marsha spent hours on this site filling out all our information, and when finished, it said it was not complete. This was extremely frustrating for Marsha, and she was never finished until we got to the airport and checked in with Air Canada. We discovered that Covid made traveling very confusing and difficult. Before returning to America, we had to get another Covid test at the airport to be cleared to enter the US. That Covid test cost us $66 each, and some Covid tests at hotels were as high as $150 each. Someone is really making money off of this.

So much for the negative part of our trip. Our first two days we stayed in Vancouver and discovered it is on the San Andreas Fault line that goes all the way down California. Fortunately, Vancouver has had very few earthquakes. Our second day, we caught a Ferry to Vancouver Island and visited Butchart Gardens, which was beautiful. The tulips and daffodils were in blossom, but all other flowers were not in bloom yet because it was still too early. Marsha shot over 100 pictures of the gorgeous flowers and grounds. We also took a bus ride to Victoria, the capital of British Columbia. The bus driver recommended a place called "Blue Fish, Red Fish" for lunch. We walked a ½ mile and had a hard time finding this place as it was a small outdoor fast-food restaurant. When I asked two young gals on the sidewalk if they knew where the restaurant was, they did not but said they would google it. Right then, a lady overheard our conversation and said follow me. I'm going down these stairs to it. That was a God thing, as this place had very little signage.

We ordered Fish and Chips, which was delicious and met Georgie from the UK, who was sitting next to us in an outdoors bar. She was wearing a running outfit, and I asked her if she ran the 10K through Victoria today? She was a runner but did not run the race. The hardest part about this day is the tour was 12 hours long, from 9 am to 9 pm.

The next day, we did a "hop on and hop off" bus tour of Vancouver. This was fun and helped us to get familiar with the city, so when we visit Vancouver again after our Alaskan cruise, we would be more familiar with it on June 4-7, 2022. We got off at Granville Island and walked through the shops. There was light rain so we stayed inside many shops.

When we stayed at the Fairmont Hotel next to where the cruise ships come in, we talked with the Concierge and got the name of a small, ma and pa restaurant, that had the best egg omelets with brie cheese and locks. The owner reminded us of the lady who starred in the movie "Chocolate" because she was exuberant to have you visit her place.

The next morning, it was time to pack up and get on the train. The only thing we did not like was this meant the bellhop would come to our room at 6:10 am to pick up our luggage. This meant we had to get up at 5:15 am so we were ready to go. The bus picked us up at 7:10 am to take us to the train station, which was 20 minutes away. Then we got off the bus and got our picture taken in front of the Rocky Mountaineer train with the Canadian flag. We loaded the train, and it left Vancouver at 8:00 am, heading towards Kamloops, a city of

150,000 and headquarters for the Rocky Mountaineer train yard. Their administration HQ is in Vancouver.

While on the train, we ate fabulous breakfasts and lunches. The dining area below our main cabin could only seat half the guests at a time (35 people), so we rotated shifts. The people in the first seating today will be in the second seating tomorrow. Breakfast menu included egg benedict, scrambled eggs, potatoes and spinach, a berry parfait, or whatever you want to order. Our new friend Bruce Latimer ordered pancakes, sausage and two eggs. You could also have more than one item so I usually added the berry parfait with my order. For drinks coffee, hot chocolate, cranberry or orange juice. At lunch time, the menu had short ribs, salmon and greens (usually oregano), salmon with rice and greens, pork chops, etc. You also ordered a drink with the meal, which I had chardonnay or merlot, and water. There was always a delicious dessert like apple pastry with a scoop of vanilla ice cream or a fabulous, rich cheese cake.

If you were in the second seating for breakfast (10:30 am), they served you a warm, tasty pastry and coffee or drink order to hold you over. The second seating for lunch was at 3:00 pm so we counted that as a dinner as well as it went to 5:00 pm. While you were waiting to have lunch, they came around with drinks of your choice and a snack, which was served in a small, square porcelain container, and you had your choice of a wonderful high-class chocolate trail mix or a salty mix. Since we ate so much on the train, Marsha and I did not need dinner, and we were fully satisfied.

The seats on the train had plenty of legroom, unlike the airplanes we fly in. Plus, there were two large bathrooms on the main level that always smelled pleasant. They had a flush knob; when pushed, it made a loud gush sound like on the cruises. It was nice to stand up and go downstairs on the spiral staircase to the outdoor platform to get fresh air and a nice platform to do stretching exercises. When there was a special photo option to take a picture of incredible scenery, several people would go outside to shoot their pictures. However, the beautiful doom cars we rode in had large windows for excellent picture-taking as long as you did not get any reflection.

Our train trip from Vancouver to Kamloops had similar scenery you would find in Colorado, much of it being brown and dry, basically a high desert. Although, it was pretty along the various rivers, including Frazier, Thomson and Columbia. The Columbia River is the longest river in North America, 1240 miles long and very wide. At spots, it looks like a lake, and there were many forts along the river, which is where British Columbia's name originates. Columbia River connects into the North West passage and travels into Oregon and eventually into the Pacific Ocean.

The explorer Simon Frazier was a gifted guide along the Frazier River and was awarded the river being named after him. He discovered Hell's Gate in 1808 on the Frazier River, which is the narrowest spot on the river, only 34 yards wide. This became a very strong waterfalls, pouring twice as much water as Niagara Falls.

Another interesting fact is the Spiral Tunnels that were built for the railroad to compensate a steep grade of 4.5% on Big Hill Trap. For 25 years, there were many accidents trying to use runaway railway sections. These were unsuccessful and it cost the railroad thousands of dollars in losses and time until finally a permanent solution was found in the Spiral Tunnels. It was considered an amazing feat blasting a 3200' tunnel through Mount Cathedral and they connected both spiral tunnels within one inch of each other. This allowed the train to travel on a grade of only 2 ½ % versus the original 4.5%. It became a major breakthrough for the Canadian railroad.

What's unbelievable is there are freight trains that are 2 ½ miles long carrying oil, lumber and various freight. Canada is very dependent upon their freight trains for a strong economy.

We witnessed many of these trains on our trip. Several times, we needed to wait on a pull-out while a freight train would pass us in the opposite direction. These delays were unpredictable and would cause us to get to our next destination later than expected. But freight trains always had the right of way. There are two major train lines in Canada: the Pacific Railway and the National Railway. They originally competed against each other but work together today. There are two rail lines along the rivers, one on each side. This allows a clear direction for both sides.

At one point in our trip, we crossed over the Continental Divide. We were at 5000', and it is the only place in North America that divides the water into eventually three oceans: Atlantic, Pacific, and Arctic. In 1885, the final spike of the railroad was pounded at "Credulity spot" covering over 3,000 miles across Canada and cost over $100 million in those days. A staggering amount today!

The two-day train trip ended in Jasper, a pristine small village in the Canadian Rockies. We stayed at the Fairmont Hotel in Jasper, and to our surprise, all the rooms were in nicely furnished cabins. As we got to our cabin, there was a "Happy Anniversary" sign in chocolate with several small pastries and Champagne. When we woke up the next morning, we were shocked that a little critter had crawled up on the table and taken several bites out of our pastries. When we reported this to the front desk, they apologized and said that, unfortunately, these mice are protected by the National Park in Jasper. We both laughed that we came all the way here only to contend with the mice problem that we have at home, having trapped over 500 mice since 1997.

The next morning, a tour bus with Brewers picked us up at 7:30 am for our scenic drive to Lake Louise. Both of us agreed that this section was the best part of the whole trip. We enjoyed seeing the beautiful Canadian Rocky Mountains which reminded us of the Swiss Alps with their jagged peaks and lots of snow. We also saw wild life like a bear, moose, big horn sheep, elk, a bald eagle with its white head, and deer. They have a custom on the buses and trains that whenever someone sees any wildlife, you are to call out, "Bear on the right." What was really funny is the people on this trip even got excited about seeing a deer, which is so common where we live it was no big deal. When we traveled on the bus between Jasper and Lake Louise, we encountered the Columbia Ice Field and Athabasca Glacier, which is 3000' high.

Lake Louise was our absolute favorite place to visit. We stayed at the Fairmont Hotel, which was fabulous, and our room had a spectacular view of Lake Louise, which was iced over and surrounded by the Rockies. We also had white wine and chocolate mousse to celebrate our anniversary, waiting for us in our room. We felt like we were royalty. AAA not only gave us two free rooms at the Fairmont Hotel in Vancouver but also a free dinner in Lake Louise at the Fairmont. We ordered a three-course Swiss Fondue meal, which was $95 Canadian dollars each. First course was the traditional cheese fondue with bread and various vegetables, then Filet Menon, which was 1" thick, but unfortunately, it was hard to chew up. This was very disappointing, and after struggling with half of it, we didn't eat the rest. They offered to give us two new cuts, but we refused since we still had the 3rd course to eat— chocolate fondue with pieces of marshmallow and fruit. The whole meal, including the tip, was paid for by Triple A. This was quite generous and we were impressed by the bonuses we received from them on this trip.

Lake Louise has a Swiss influence because in the early 1900s, there were fatal hiking accidents in the area, and it received bad press. So, they hired experienced Swiss hikers to help them through this difficult time. This turned things around, and Lake Louise became a popular tourist destination again. It is in the providence of Alberta, Canada and the time zone changed from PTZ to MST, which is one hour ahead. There are numerous avalanches in this area, which makes it dangerous for hikers. We saw a major tunnel for the train to go through under the avalanche. At the same place down from the tunnel is a major dam of dirt to protect the road from the same avalanche. The railway also had tripwires to notify them of large rocks that would endanger the railway. The area is also filled with numerous glaciers that cut out major valleys versus rivers that carve out narrow canyons. Today, there are beautiful rivers for white water rafting and fishing. Many of the areas have clear blue, ice-cold water coming right off the glaciers.

This is also a Salmon country in which the female Salmon would lay up to 4000 eggs in a nest. After a full cycle of traveling all the way to the Pacific Ocean and back only 8-10 of the Salmon would survive of the 4000. The Salmon has the unique ability to adjust from fresh water to salt water and back again. We witnessed an Osprey bird and a Bald Eagle fighting over a lake for a Salmon. The Osprey has a wing span of 6' and is an excellent hunter of fish. They have a black and white head in contrast to the Bald Eagle with its white head. At one time the eagle was considered to be a pest and became almost extinct. Both birds build their nests at the top of trees. The Bald Eagles are said to be scavengers and try to steal food from other birds. It is also lazy and will take over others' nests rather than build their own. At least, this is the version in Canada. I can't imagine why America would make the eagle to be its national symbol if this was true.

There was a question about beaver dams. The reason we did not see any beavers is because they are nocturnal. It is interesting that their homes have a mud room at their entrance to shake off their mud for the rest of their home. It is kind of like people who ask visitors to remove their shoes to help keep their house clean. They said this is like Canadian hospitality.

We learned that indigenous people used limestone to make their hot tea. They would put a limestone in the fire, get it hot, and then move it to a pot of water in rawhide. The limestone rock would heat up the water then they would add pine needles in it, which are rich in vitamin C. A hand full of pine needles is the equivalent of four oranges. They might also add green tea and chamomile.

We traveled from Lake Louise to Banff, which is a small village of 10,000 people. There is a rule that you must reside in Banff in order to own a home. This rule keeps foreigners from trying to buy a summer home and only be a snow bird. This has kept the population of 10,000 in check. Banff became popular in 1885 when they discovered hot springs, which were inviting for people who were suffering from polio and other illnesses. The hot sulfur was believed to be a cure for many who suffered with sickness. We enjoyed taking the Banff Gondola, which took us 7546' above the town for an incredible 360-degree view of the valley and the surrounding Canadian Rockies. It was a very smooth ride, seats 4-6 people and helped offset the fear of heights for even the most squeamish rider. This was breathtaking and a highlight of our tour.

From Banff, our train went back to Kamloops and Vancouver. For people who do not prefer to do the round trip back to Vancouver, they can choose to catch a motor coach from Banff to Calgary which is 90 miles away. This would save two more days on the train and approximately $3,000 for two people.

Our total cost was $13,000, so it would have only been $10,000, and then we would have flown home from Calgary. We learned that Calgary has a population of 1.5 million people and hosts the famous annual "rodeo stampede." Both Marsha and I would choose to do this route, as two days on the train is plenty of time. Plus, this would save you another hotel bill in Kamloops.

When we registered with AAA, we did not know this was an option. We also did not know that two days on the train would be sufficient. Plus, this would have saved us two days of having to get up extra early for baggage pick-up and bus to the train station. Those days were very long. Most Europeans fly to Calgary and then do the reverse trip to Vancouver and add an Alaskan Cruise.

We learned that Canada was formed in 1867 with a total population of only three million people. In western Canada, there was a gold rush that brought many Americans from San Francisco after their gold rush ceased. Another fascinating fact was Stoney Creek Bridge which the Rocky Mountaineer train crossed. This bridge is 300' high over the river and is the second-highest bridge in the world. It was originally a wooden bridge built in 1879 and then replaced with a steel bridge built on the wooden bridge in 1907. This bridge was replaced in 1929 with another steel bridge built for support on top of the other steel bridge. This bridge is one of the incredibly, picturesque scenes on our journey.

We also passed by Sicamous Lake, which is the Canadian houseboat capital because of its enormous size. Unlike Lake Powell in the US, which is facing a severe drought, it is full of water and 500' deep. Its length is some 30 miles long. There are black bears around this area. One of the unique facts of these animals is after their hibernating is complete they eat a plant called "Skunk Cabbage," which is a yellow flower and acts like a laxative to help clean them out.

Our bus drivers call bicyclists "Meals on Wheels." The Rocky Mountaineer package used Brewster tour buses, which were very comfortable and had a restroom in the back. The bus drivers were very knowledgeable of the area they drove through and, besides being excellent drivers, were also good tour guides and shared many interesting stories and facts. They shared things like, "Do you know what happens when people jump into icy waters. A Canadian Sex Change." They also shared about Lake Miniwauka, which means "many Spirits of the water." It is like Minnesota, which means "many lakes." There is a story about a lake monster of Lake Miniwauka that scared numerous visitors away. Finally, a clever entrepreneur created a large lake monster with a human head and a fishtail and showed the tourists he had captured it so that tourists would once again visit Lake Miniwauka.

All and all, this was one incredible train trip in Canada, definitely worth our time and money. It was a very romantic and fun vacation as we celebrated our 54th anniversary.

Kate Perkin's Wedding

June 2, 2022

Since we both got Covid, we canceled our trip to Alaska once again, the third time. Hopefully, we will go in 2023 and celebrate our 55th anniversary. When we talked with Paul and Jenny and told them we would not be coming to Anchorage in 2022, they said, "Try to come to Kate's wedding in California near San Jose." We discussed it and decided to fly out there on the morning of June 2 and attend the wedding at 7 pm. This became a double hitter as we would stay in San Jose and celebrate grandpa's 95th birthday on June 5. Because we did not make our flight reservation until three weeks out, it cost us $850, but it was worth it.

We got dressed in our fancy clothes and borrowed Grandpa's van to drive 30 miles to the wedding in Woodside. We used our GPS to find this spot which was way up in the mountains at a very isolated place. After driving on the freeway past Palo Alto and Menlo Park, we got off the exit that became a very narrow and twisty road called Old La Honda Road. It seemed like it went on forever and was only wide enough for 1 ½ vehicles. This was quite stressful driving and extremely slow. Fortunately, we left at 5:25 pm, so we arrived by 6:30, which gave us a chance to visit with Paul and Jenny when she wasn't running around doing last-minute decorations.

It was great to see both of them. Paul was in his Best Dress Air Force Uniform with all his ribbons and paraphernalia. He looked great and was still able to fit into his uniform that he hadn't worn in eight years. Many former military members put on weight and are not able to wear their uniforms anymore. It was a small destination wedding with only 50-60 people in attendance. The chairs were placed outside on the grass that was overlooking the San Francisco Bay area. Paul and Jenny both brought Kate down the aisle which was special. The minister was their young youth pastor. Paul said it was his first wedding. He did okay but forgot to include the bride and groom vows which are central to a wedding ceremony. Oh well, life is not perfect, but they were in love, and their marriage happened.

One of the best things that happened was during the reception after the best man and maid of honor shared their words. When anyone else was invited to come forward and share words with the bride and groom, Paul came forward as the father of the bride to share his personal comments. He closed his words by reading from I Corinthians 13 the words on love. I said to Marsha, "And this is our Atheist Cadet at the Air Force Academy 32 years ago." Paul is now an on-fire Christian who takes his family to Mount Hermon Christian Conference Grounds for a week retreat every summer.

We left at 10 pm and drove home a different route to avoid Old La Honda Road. We took Skyline Drive which was a scenic road that parallels the Bay Area and Santa Clara County. It was up in the mountains above the valley. I later told people it was a perfect road for a sports car but not for a van. There were several curves and hair pin turns and lots of ups and downs. This road was better than Old La Honda Road, being at least two lanes, but it, too, was very stressful.

Part of the problem is the dashboard lights were very dim, and I could not read how fast I was going. It was also very dark and when a car would come behind us, it was quite blinding. The road was so twisty that there were very few spots I could pull over to let them pass. This road felt like we were on it forever, too, 25 miles, until it finally dumped us into Saratoga, which got us to Campbell Ave and home. It was definitely the more direct route, but very intense driving. The wedding was a wonderful celebration, and it was great to see the Perkin family. We had not seen Paul for over 15 years. We put $60 of gas in the van at $6.59/gallon at 11:00 pm and finally got home at 11:15 pm. We were exhausted since we got up at 3:45 am to catch an early flight from Colorado Springs. Traveling is definitely tiring especially in light of the Covid pandemic.

Cheyenne Mountain Zoo

On June 22, 2022, Marsha and I, along with Jewel and Mae, Chanelle, Sierra and Brooklyn, went to the Cheyenne Mountain Zoo. It was Chanelle's Father's Day gift to me, which was very generous. The cost of the zoo is now $30 minus a $3 Military discount each. Fortunately, she had a year's pass for four tickets, so she only had to pay for one child ticket plus ours. It was a beautiful day, and the temperature was 70 degrees at 10 am. Since we got there at 10 am when it opened, it was not very crowded. By the end of our time, four hours later, there were numerous people, so we hit it right.

It was so much fun going with our three granddaughters and watching their excitement in seeing all the different animals and birds. The two exhibits that were our favorite were the elephants and giraffes. At the elephant area, we witnessed an elephant pick-up a large log with its trunk. Then, it pressed it up against a pole and proceeded to strip off the bark with its strong tusk. After stripping off the bark, the elephant proceeded to put the bark in its mouth with its trunk. There were numerous logs on the near-by ground that had been debarked. This must give the elephant incredible fiber.

Next we saw 14-15 giraffes that were begging for lettuce to eat from the people. I learned that this zoo has the largest concentration of giraffes of any zoo. They have leaves of lettuce for sale for $3 for a single helping and $5 for a double portion. At first, we did not have any lettuce, and Sierra and Brooklyn would find scraps of small pieces of lettuce on the ground. They presented those small pieces to the giraffes, but most giraffes wanted bigger pieces, which was frustrating for the girls. Finally, Jewel was kind enough to go and buy some large pieces of lettuce, and then the fun began.

We had giraffes coming in our direction to get the lettuce with their long tongues. Their tongues were 1-11/2 feet in length. As you would hold the lettuce out there, the giraffe would come and grab it with its long tongue and often get your hand as well. The girls loved feeling the slimy tongue and seeing the giraffe take their lettuce. Of course, this event was too important not to get on pictures. So all of us got in the action and laughed at what was happening.

This day at the zoo was very memorable, and everyone had lots of fun. By 2:30 pm, we were all tired, and the temperature in the sun was quite warm, so it was time to go home. Goodbye animals, until next time!

Scary Chest Pain

After doing so well from the brain surgery in September 2021, I had a scary event the following summer. I had just finished working on the computer for two hours when Marsha returned home. As I stood up, suddenly, I had severe chest pain on the left side of my shoulder. I had never felt this before, and it was disconcerting. I told Marsha about it, and she told me to lie down upstairs and see if it goes away. In the meantime, she tried calling our primary care doctor, Adam Robinson, to discuss this with him. At first she was not able to reach him but left a message. Thirty minutes later, he called us and asked me several questions. Where was the pain? Was it a sharp stabbing pain? After taking a baby aspirin 30 minutes ago, has the pain decreased? Since I told him that the pain had not decreased, he suggested having Marsha take me to the Emergency at the Hospital and tell them that my doctor recommended that I come in because I was having chest pains. As a result, when we arrived at the hospital, they quickly took me in ahead of others who were waiting.

I ended up going to Memorial North Hospital, which specializes in heart patients. When we got there at 7 pm, there were only a few people in the Emergency room. The first thing they did was give me an EKG and then an x-ray on my chest. After that, they took blood from me to check the heart ensign, which would show them if I was having a heart attack. I met with the nurse who was from Ukraine. Her family is still there, and she was very concerned with the war with Russia and the safety of her family. Marsha and I were able to share my healing which encouraged her to believe. We even had prayers for her and her family, which she deeply appreciated. When the doctor came him, he assured me he didn't think I was having a heart attack but needed me to stay for two hours after the first blood test to take it again. We stayed in the back room until the doctor came again and said the EKG, x-ray, and blood tests all looked good, so you may go home. However, I want to refer you to a cardiologist just a caution.

My primary care doctor referred me to a cardiologist whom I visited a month later. He wanted to give me three different tests to check on my heart. These happened in three different appointments. The first one was a Stress Test while walking on a treadmill and being all wired up to show the health of the heart. This test took 12 minutes starting out on a fairly flat level and then after three minutes to increase the speed and elevate the lift level. After each three minutes, the test repeated this process. At first, it is very easy to breathe and not much exertion. But by the time they had your heart working hard because of the intensity of the exercise, you were ready to have this test to be over. When they reached your peak effort, they immediately laid you down on the table to monitor the reaction of your heart and how fast it can recover.

After the Stress Test, they did a calcium test on my heart to see if my heart collects plaque in its arteries and vessels. They give you a score from 0 to 100. Zero being the best and 100 being the worse. This test can predict the possibility of having a heart attack. Having a score of "0" means that your chances of having a heart attack are very minimal. My score came back "0," which was great news. They also told me my Stress Test and EKG results were quite good. This was comforting to know, especially having dad die from a massive heart attack at age 77. Since I was now 74, Dr. Adam Robinson said it was important to play it safe and to go through all these heart measures. I am very grateful for a healthy heart. Thank you, God!!

Marriage Workshop

Oct 2022

Marsha and I attended an intensive marriage workshop by New Life ministries called "Intimacy in Marriage" on Oct 21-23, 2022. It was offered at a hotel in Dallas, Texas. When I asked Marsha what she wanted for her birthday, she responded, "I want to attend the "Intimacy in Marriage" workshop. Since her birthday was on October 21, she got her wish and we attended this event over her birthday.

When we arrived, we had no idea how many couples would be attending this workshop. 62 couples appeared at this event of all ages. It was advertised for all marriages: good marriages that want to be great, struggling marriages that need help, and marriages that need a tune-up. After 54 years of marriage, we felt that we had a good marriage but wanted it to be even better. The workshop was intensive because it was like drinking from a fire hose. We had six sessions in the lecture hall for one hour each. Plus, we had five small group meetings with four couples and a facilitator for 1 ½ hours. The real work happened in small groups where we applied the concepts that were taught in the lectures.

Marsha and I had fortunately read the book they sent us ahead of the workshop, which really helped us understand the concepts better and not be confused. Some couples came without reading anything beforehand and were struggling to keep up. The lecture leaders, Milan and Kay Yurkovich, were married for 50+ years and are part of New Life Ministries. The workshop started on Friday, October 23, at 3 pm and went to 8:30 pm. On Saturday, it started at 9:00 am and ran straight through until 9 pm. The closing day on Sunday started at 9 am until noon. We then had an airplane to catch at 3 pm to fly home to Denver. It was an exhausting weekend physically but, relationally very refreshing.

We met three other couples in our small group and the facilitator more in-depth. We especially enjoyed getting to know Molly and Billy in our group. Billy had been through another New Life Ministry workshop entitled "Every Man's Battle" on pornography. Through this workshop he became a Christian and is a new person. As a result, he wanted to improve his marriage and encouraged Molly to "Come and See." She was not a Christian, and she came out of respect for him.

Probably the biggest takeaway from the workshop was the power childhood imprints have in our lives. We all are influenced by our past childhood which influences both our conscience and sub-conscience mind. These past scars can become trigger points that can play havoc in a marriage relationship. Many times, the conflicts between husband and wife are rooted in our childhood imprints. Trying to understand what childhood imprints we have can help defuse any heated arguments. This takes a lot of work and is often not easy to discover. But if one can embrace the problem from childhood, it can bring greater understanding and resolution to the problem. We also learned how important it is to have boundaries as a protection of one's time and resources. As hard as it is to say no, it is critical to enjoy a balanced life. One of the practical plans that we have put in place is to have more date nights.

Advent Season

The end of November starts the advent season to celebrate the coming of Christ. It is the time to reflect on God's goodness to us and get ready for Christmas. This is an unusual period that is very unique for the church. It always happens right after Thanksgiving and is a time to be grateful. Thankful for all that God has done and will be doing in our lives.

The songs we sing are unique to the era and completely different than Christmas hymns. It is a time that helps us get ready for Christmas and what Christ has done in our world and our lives. Help us, Oh Lord, to be ever grateful to you for life and health and the many good things you do for us.

I had the privilege of preaching for five Sundays during the Advent Season for First Presbyterian Church in Pueblo, Colorado, in 2022. Their senior pastor had just resigned, and the church needed someone to fill the pulpit before an Interim Pastor started in January. Since I had been the Interim Pastor for this church in 2015-2016 for nine months, they wanted me to come and fill the void. I felt God calling me to help this church during this critical time. I had the privilege of sharing my miracle of healing and challenged the church with the message of hope during this time of anxiety. What a joy to witness God's Spirit moving among them, and there were even numerous people who committed their lives to Jesus. This was a great celebration of the true meaning of Advent.

Huge Benefits from the Air Force

When I joined the Air Force as a meager Captain back in 1981, I had no idea of the many future benefits that were awaiting me and my family. I was simply looking to get an opportunity to minister to young men and women in the Air Force. After interviewing several Air Force chaplains, I was convinced there was something special about joining this elite group of people. I had always admired pilots as a boy growing up, and I remember going to Moffat Field and watching the Blue Angels put on a special air show. Although the Blue Angels were from the Navy, I did not make the distinction between what military service they were. In my mind, they were only fantastic pilots who flew with incredible precision and speed. I remember being quite impressed. However, as I grew older, I knew that I could not be a pilot because I did not have 20-20 vision. At that time, I did not know that God had a different path for me to follow in order to become a chaplain and a sky pilot in the Air Force. Who would have thought this was the journey God had carved out for me.

In order to be an ordained Presbyterian minister, you need to have not only your college degree but also a Master of Divinity degree from an accredited seminary. Years before thinking about going into the Air Force, I attended Fuller Theological Seminary in Pasadena to attain my Master of Divinity Degree from 1970-1973. My plans at that time were to become a part-time youth director at Knox Presbyterian Church during my last two years in seminary to help with the tuition. I ended up staying at the church for ten years as an Assistant Pastor, Associate Pastor and my last 18 months as the Interim Pastor. After talking with a Navy officer at our church who encouraged me to become a military chaplain, I applied to become an Air Force chaplain. Marsha and I went to Washington, DC, to be interviewed by the Presbyterian Council of Chaplain board. The good news is I qualified to become a Presbyterian Air Force Chaplain. However, no active duty Air Force chaplain slots were available, so I became a Reserve Air Force chaplain while serving at First Presbyterian Church in Colorado Springs for four years. After this time in the Reserve, I became an active duty chaplain, and our family moved to San Bernardino, California and served at Norton Air Force Base for three years. This was my critical beginning to an incredible Air Force Career that lasted for 26 wonderful years.

During my years in the Air Force, we were blessed with fabulous benefits that unfolded through my career and now retirement. There was a stable salary plus tax-free housing and food allowance. Access to the commissary, an equivalent of a large military grocery store, with excellent food cost savings on certain items. Discounts for playing golf and going bowling were available. Free usage of large gyms, swimming pools and running tracks were offered. If one had the patience and time, Space Available to fly to many areas worldwide on military jets was offered to you and your dependents for only $10 each way. We took advantage of this to Hawaii and also to Anchorage, Alaska, with our family when the girls were young.

Besides all the inside benefits of the Air Force, numerous discounts are offered to military members in the community. For example, Home Depot and Lowes offer a 10% discount on any purchase. You can also receive a 10% discount at IHOP, Apple Bees, Dennys and many more eateries. These discounts all add up and help your budget. Often, companies in a military town will offer a 10% discount on home repairs and other improvements.

Going further outside your local community, there are discounts offered to military members like purchasing tickets for Disneyland and Disney World. These are significant discounts of 40-50% off the regular ticket price. You can also receive a large benefit by staying at a military resort like Bellows in Hawaii for $25/night for a beach cabin or the military hotel on Waikiki for a significant reduction in price. This is also true of Shades of Green resort next to Disney World in Florida. We have stayed there numerous times with Mae, Jewel and Christian Magoon and found it to be an excellent place to stay for a very reasonable price. These are only a sample of some of the benefits we have been blessed to receive. Now that I am retired, the above discounts continue, and I am blessed to receive a generous pension that we receive every month. This has allowed us to enjoy financial freedom during some tumultuous financial times. It is wonderful to have a solid paycheck coming in no matter what is happening in our uncertain world.

Another fabulous benefit is the medical and dental insurance. When on active duty, your medical and dental are 100% covered. Once retired, Tricare for Life supplements Medicare insurance for a fabulous medical coverage. When I was seeing three neurologists and having many tests to determine what was wrong, this insurance covered 100% of the medical charges. Then, when I went to the Mayo Clinic in Phoenix, Arizona, after four long years in 2021, all the medical charges were covered. This included my brain surgery to insert a shunt for my hydrocephalus, water on the brain. It's hard enough to go through dangerous brain surgery without having to worry about financial charges. This is also true of our dental coverage, which covers 100% of cleaning and X-rays and 50% coverage on crowns. This costs us a $50-a-month deduction through Delta Dental.

Top Favorite Sayings for Life

In life, there are many suggestions on how to have a successful life. Unfortunately, some are not relevant and, if followed, could offer disastrous results. There are many people whose goal in life is to scam others in order to get rich. Sadly, this is a billion-dollar industry that hurts many innocent victims. It is important to be vigilant and not fall into get-rich-quick schemes. Over my lifetime, I have come up with some very practical sayings that have helped me stay on the right path. Many of them are Biblically based and have brought me wisdom in my life. I want to share them with you now. The following ones are not all-inclusive but will give you an idea of key ones that have helped me.

1.   <u>Take the High Road:</u> I learned this lesson when I was an Air Force Chaplain. I attended many training events. One of the speakers who I highly respected, told us, "People, in your Air Force career, let me encourage you to always take the high road." When you are faced with a difficult decision that involves money, never cheat the government or your colleagues. It is important to lean on the side of generosity rather than cheapness. When dealing with a difficult person who has hurt you, try to give them the benefit of the doubt. Sometimes, that means having to forgive them even when they are wrong. When in a heated debate, try to be loving and kind when there is strong disagreement. It doesn't do any good to win a battle and lose the war.

2.   <u>Let Go, Let God:</u> When I was going through a very difficult time in my life, I had a wonderful Catholic Priest friend, Father Frank Faucet, who told me to "let go and let God." I was angry over being treated unfairly by a boss, and it was eating away at me. Father Faucet knew what I was going

through because of a similar situation in his life. He told me the only way he found a peaceful resolution was to turn it over to God and let it go. He said, "Dave, you need to reach down deep and forgive the offender so it no longer eats away at you." That was sage advice, and eventually, I was able to forgive and move on.

3. <u>Treat others the way you want to be treated:</u> When I remember that we are all created in the image of God with value and significance, it helps me to treat people with respect and love. This is a key ingredient that is sadly missing in our society. The opposite of this is to be selfish, prideful and out to get everything for me. This is never the way God intended us to live our lives, and if we choose this route, it only causes pain and brokenness in relationships. The Golden rule, "to love one another as God loves us," is the best advice for us individually and for society as a whole.

4. <u>If it's worth doing, it is worth doing right:</u> This was a principle that my grandparents and parents instilled in me. This is the idea of putting your best foot forward on all projects and tasks. It is not the idea of perfectionism that leads one down a wrong rabbit trail. But rather to be proud of any job you are asked to do. The result of that job is a reflection on you. Whether it was washing and waxing the car, cutting the grass, vacuuming the carpets, washing the dishes or anything else, it is important to do an excellent job. Even when others are not watching, God is and expects the best from you.

5. <u>Life is short, eat desserts first:</u> When I was visiting the Base Commander's office as an Air Force Chaplain, I noticed he had a plaque on his desk that said, "Life is short, eat desserts first." At first, it may sound a bit comical, but when you give it more thought, there is much truth in this saying. It is much more than just satisfying your sweet tooth by eating desserts, but it means prioritizing your life and accomplishing what is

really important and not getting sidetracked with less temporal things. Life is short and only offers us so many hours to make the best of our journey. It can also mean making sure you plan the important things to put in your schedule for yourself and your family. The hectic pace of life can keep you from reaching your goals or taking away critical time with your family. It goes along with the idea of making the first thing, the first thing, and not settling for the second best.

6. <u>God so loved the world that He did not send a committee:</u> When I was working at Knox Presbyterian Church in Los Angeles, my senior pastor had this sign on his desk. I fell in love with these words. Although the church relies on committees to help get the work of ministry done, sometimes working on a committee can be more trouble than it is worth. This happens when people get in power and try to run things their way and do not accept the ideas of others. This can lead to arguments and wasting time with no positive production happening. People's feelings often get hurt, and sometimes even leave the church. In contrast to a committee, God sent Jesus which is a breath of fresh air.

7. <u>Blessed is the person who has an honest mechanic:</u> Having a mechanic who you can trust to take the best care of your car is important. A mechanic who will only repair what is necessary and charge you a fair price is foundational. Everyone has to take their cars in to get them tuned up and get repairs completed. This is just part of life. When you know you can trust the mechanic with your car and you are not going to be cheated, it gives you comfort and trust. This can lower your stress level in this essential area.

8. <u>Better to light one candle than to curse the darkness:</u> This is true and can be applied to many areas of one's life. I used it in a sermon when talking about a broken relationship, friction on the job, financial loss or driving on the freeway

when someone cuts you off. It is a very profound motto that can help you do what is right and not go down the wrong road. I believe this motto is what Jesus calls us to do every day of our lives.

9. <u>More blessed to give than to receive:</u> This comes right out of the scriptures and is something that Jesus wants us to follow. Unfortunately, there are people who are takers and only care about what they can get out of life. We have all experienced these kinds of people who we don't enjoy being around. All they care about is "me" and what I can get from others. They make friends on how they can use them not care about them. They are narcissistic and their whole world revolves around only them. These people do not make good friends and are hard to trust. In contrast, Jesus wants us to be generous with our time, talent and resources and share them with others in need. There is great joy in giving in a friendship, charity and loving others.

10.   <u>No limit to what can be done if you don't care who gets the credit</u>: One of the great things about brainstorming in a session is everyone is invited to suggest their creative ideas. There are no wrong ideas, and everyone is invited to participate. When this kind of meeting takes place, it can produce many good ideas because everyone is on the same team and working together. Synergy is taking place, and everyone is important in this process. There is no one person who dominates or dictates the results but wisely allows the group to function as a whole. When people's egos are put on the shelf, good things happen. One of the central ingredients in this process is for people to display humility.

11.   <u>Building wealth is a slow process</u>: There are no good get-rich-quick schemes. If it is too good to be true, it probably is. This is one of the deceptive plays of evil to draw you into a conversation or room that is promising the moon.

These kinds of people are usually fast talkers who prey upon people who are often senior citizens who cannot afford what they are offering. They are usually slick in their presentation and will try to make you feel guilty if you say no to their sales gimmick. In contrast to them, true wealth usually comes through years of wise investing in real estate, equities or other avenues that are solid investments. We all want to have more money quickly. But when we fall prey to this thinking, it usually ends up in disaster.

Alaskan Trip

(May 28-June 11, 2023)

After three years of cancellations, we finally got to take our dream trip to Alaska. In 2020, our trip was cancelled because of Covid in the U.S. In 2021, Covid in Canada cancelled it. Last year, in 2022, we both got Covid after our Canadian Rocky Mountaineer train ride. Finally, in 2023, we were healthy enough to enjoy going to Alaska, and Covid was not an issue. Each year, we had to go through the hassle of cancelling our trips, which included flights, hotels and cruises. We spent hours on the telephone and computer to start over again. This was quite frustrating.

Our plans included a trip to fly to Anchorage, Alaska, to visit Paul and Jenny Perkins for three days, doing a land tour of Mount Denali for three days, catching a Princess Cruise in Whittier, Alaska and doing a 7-day cruise down the inland passage, and finally taking our good friends Darrell and Sharon Johnson in Vancouver, British Columbia out for brunch. This is one of the reasons it was so difficult to reschedule for three years in a row. We flew from Denver, Colorado, to Anchorage, Alaska, at 7:30 pm and arrived at 11 pm their time and 1 am Denver time. What was amazing was that it wasn't dark yet. The flight was five hours long and we got to bed at 3 am Colorado time.

Paul was one of our first Air Force Academy Cadets whom we sponsored for four years in 1990. To sponsor a cadet was to adopt them as part of your family on weekends when they can get off base. This included picking them up, taking them home, feeding them meals, letting them use your washer and dryer and just being part of your family. It is a big commitment but is very rewarding. Paul graduated in 1994 and went to pilot training for a year. He became an A 10 pilot, flying ground support for the Army. After serving in the Air Force for 20 years, he retired from the Air Force and flew for Southwest Airlines for the next four years. Paul always wanted to live in Alaska and became a pilot for Federal Express which has a hub in Anchorage.

On our first day with the Perkins, Paul invited us to go flying in his private airplane because the weather was good. It's good that we went that day as the weather became poor the next two days. Paul took us for a 90 minute flight over Anchorage and two glaciers. We flew 300 feet over the glaciers at 100 mph. Because of the wind coming off the mountains, the flight at times was bumpy, as Paul would say to Jenny, "Are you okay?" She would respond, "Yes, but I don't like it." What a fantastic flight we were blessed with and we both agreed it was the best excursion possible. Flying with Paul and Jenny was certainly a *highlight* of our trip.

On the last night with Paul and Jenny, Jenny shared with us what she was creating for Young Life. She volunteers as a mentor for young, single mothers. We were shocked to learn Jenny had created a full year of devotions for her area to use. She spent hours putting this together, which was masterfully done. We were so proud of her for sharing her creativity in this ministry.

We then stayed at Captain Cook hotel, named after the founder of Anchorage, before catching a bus the next morning to travel to Mount McKinley Lodge at 2,000 feet elevation. On the way to the lodge, it was not only raining but snowing on June 1 our anniversary. This was our 55th wedding anniversary that we were celebrating. In order to catch our bus, they required us to have our luggage ready to pick up at 6 am. Unfortunately, our luggage was not delivered to our rooms at McKinley Lodge until 7 pm. We discovered on our trip in Alaska that Russia sold Alaska to America in October 1867 for $7.2 million, or less than two cents an acre. Russia made a huge mistake selling Alaska rich in gold and oil.

The next day, we stayed at Mt. Denali Lodge and took a 4 ½ hour tour of the wilderness, which was worth it. Although we were on a school bus because of the regulations in a national park, we had an incredible tour and saw many wild animals. We saw caribou, moose, a black porcupine, a brown grizzly bear, bald eagles and then God brought the sunshine out, and we were blessed to see Mt. Denali off in the distance 75 miles away. It had a blueish tent, overshadowing the white snow. They say seeing Mt. Denali, "the great one, the high one," doesn't happen very often.

On Saturday, June 3, we boarded our Princess train for a 9 ½ hour trip to Whittier, where we will board our Princess Cruise ship, The Majestic. It is one of their larger ships holding 3500 passengers. Our train ride through Alaska reminded us of the train ride on the Rocky Mountaineer in Canada. The cars were similar, with a dome car on top and a dining car below. One of the main differences was the train ride was bumpier due to rails built on permafrost.

One of the prettiest sights on the trip was "Hurricane Gulch." It was an incredible trestle built in 1921 to allow the rail tracks to be built over a 300-foot gulch and river below. We also went through a 2 ½ mile tunnel through a high mountain. This was another amazing engineering feat. We learned that there are over three million lakes of 20 acres minimum size. When we got to Whittier at 6 pm, all 500 passengers got off the train to go through security to board the ship. This took over 30 minutes and was like being in a long line at Disneyland. Besides this negative experience and the disorganized way of serving lunch, the overall land experience was well worth it. Another of our "bucket lists" completed.

Home Fireworks

July 4, 2023

To celebrate the 4th of July in 2023, we decided to have a BBQ with hot dogs and brats and invited the Muros, Magoons, and our neighbors, the Septers, here for lunch at noon. Marsha and I began working for this event the day before and got the patio washed off, washed and put a film on the spa top, and put out special flags in our front and backyard. In addition, we prepared food ahead of time, vacuumed the house, set up special tables in the backyard and prepared well for this celebration to honor our country's birthday. America is so blessed with so much that we truly have much to be grateful for: not only freedom but riches beyond our needs.

We were so excited to host this special occasion with 14 people and we were fully ready by 10 am. However, Marsha decided to wash some windows in the back of the house to spruce it up. This was a great idea until she lost her balance, tripped over the stairs to the hot tub and fell straight on her back and the back of her head on the hard concrete.

This was a horrible accident that happened. As I was vacuuming close to the back door, I suddenly heard Marsha cry out, "Dave, help me." As I looked out the glass door, Marsha was lying on the concrete, holding her head in a pool of blood from the fall. This sight scared me to death as I thought she had cracked her skull open. I quickly got a hand towel and rushed out to help her put pressure on her skull.

At first, I thought, "Oh, no. I better take her to the emergency." After putting pressure on the wound, it finally slowed down the bleeding. I also got an ice pack and put it on the wound as she sat in the massage chair. I gave her 1000mg of Tylenol to help with the pain. Fortunately, the swelling was outside the head much better than inward swelling.

She had a large goose egg on the back of her head. The bleeding continued to slow down, which was good.

When Seth Septer, who is a pediatrician, came over for lunch with his family, he looked at the gash and said she was fortunate as it was less than an inch long, so no stitches were necessary. The other good news is her vision was still normal, and there was no concussion. I told Marsha, "Your 96-year-old dad falls down every two weeks because of balance and weakness issues. We don't need you to add to these falls." I also told Dr. Septer, "It is a good thing that Marsha has a hard head." He laughed. Marsha was brilliant enough to wear a headband to keep pressure on the gauze. We are really glad that Marsha's guardian angel surrounded her that day. Believe it or not, we were able to continue to have the BBQ and celebration of July 4 with lots of gratitude.

The Miracle Baby

After Scott and Star got married on May 15, 2021, they both decided that it was important to have a child. So they tried to get Star pregnant, but it did not happen. They then moved on to plan B and tried to adopt a baby. They began this process one year after their wedding. What they did not realize is how complicated a process this is to complete. After being interviewed and creating a booklet to represent themselves, their booklet would be sent to the birth mom and dad. The birth parents would review several booklets and then make a decision about who they wanted to raise their new baby. Just to get started with an adoption agency, it could take several months and $4,000.

What is amazing is the total expense to adopt a child can be from $50,000 to over $100,000. This is an outrageous sum of money for new parents to commit to. This money covers the adoption agency and classes required, social workers, placement cost, administration fees, lawyer fees, money to cover the birth mom's expenses for the first three months, and several other fees. I feel this total expense is criminal and discourages potential parents from applying for a baby. How can most parents cover this expense without going into debt?

Fortunately, our close friend Dominique told Star and Scott about a program called Both Hands. Since Dominique is a widow, she was very familiar with this program that helps both orphans and widows. The couple would find a needy widow who would like a group of people to come to her home and do anything she needs help with. Star and Scott found a widow in Elizabeth, Colorado, named Terri, who was willing to be part of this program. So, they sent out a letter asking people to volunteer their time on a Saturday to do manual labor. Twenty-Four adults and six children came to help by stripping the wallpaper on the kitchen, patching up holes, and painting it a warm yellow that Terri loves. She has wanted this done for years but could not afford it. We also took down a 50 feet wall of large bricks that was three feet high and falling over. The workers built a new foundation under the bricks and stacked them up again. This produced a new wall that was no longer leaning over. The third project was to cut down 23 dead scrub oak trees and haul them away to the dump. Since Terri lives on six acres of land, this improvement looks great. We also washed windows and cleaned the house. It's amazing how much good work was accomplished in a short time.

The other half of this equation of Both Hands is to ask your friends and family not only to help with volunteering time for the widow's project but to consider donating money to help fund the new baby. They also ask for people to support them with their prayers. As a result of a fantastic community of family and friends, over $71,000 came in to support Scott and Star in their adoption process. What was amazing is this amount was exactly the expenses it cost them to adopt Skyla. This was certainly another important piece of the miracle of getting Skyla. To begin their new chapter with Skyla debt-free is miraculous! This was another wink from God this was the baby He had picked out for them. Congratulations!!!

After Scott and Star started this process of adoption, they received almost 20 rejections before a birth mom and dad chose them to become the new parents. These many rejections were very difficult as Star and Scott would get their hopes up that this might be the one for us. One of the things they discovered was if the baby was out of state, the birth parents would often choose a couple who lived in their state so they could stay in touch. Finally, after 18 months of applying, a birth mom and dad who lived in Denver, Colorado, close to Scott and Star, chose them to be the new parents of their baby girl. The fact that Star is 46 and Scott 49 was not an issue for them. They liked the fact that Scott and Star are Christians and young at heart and body.

Skyla is now four months old and is as cute a baby as one could hope for. Unlike most new babies who only sleep 2-3 hours at a time at night, Skyla soon started sleeping 3-4 hours before waking up at night. Now she is sleeping 7-10 hours a night which is such a gift for Scott and Star. They are not only blessed with a healthy baby but one who allows her parents to get good sleep. This is critical since Scott started a full time job with Valor High School two months ago. Four weeks ago, Star started going back to her counseling practice 20 hours a week after a four-month maternity leave. This excellent sleeping pattern of Skyla has allowed her parents to function well.

Skyla has brought so much happiness into the Peluso's home and extended family. She is very alert when awake and loves playing with her many toys. She melts your heart when she smiles and is already trying to talk. Skyla loves standing up next to something and just learned how to roll over from her back to her front. There is something new that she is learning every day. Star is great about sending the family a text video each morning sharing Skyla's beautiful, "good morning family smile." Star and Scott are fantastic parents and love playing with her and feeding her many bottles each day. They are both very happy parents and Skyla is being raised in a loving home. Having Skyla is such a great blessing from God to both of them and their family. We love having another sweet, loving granddaughter in our family.

Trip to Branson, MO

December, 2023

Our first trip to Branson, MO, was in April 2022, in which we saw the musical "Jesus" at the Sight and Sound Theater. We were very impressed with the acting, stage set-up, music and all else. We knew we would be back to see another performance in the future. We also got to visit with our friends, Nancy and Don Ummel, from Arkansas. Since doing this trip was on my bucket list, it was a dream come true.

Our second trip to Branson happened on Dec 4-10, 2023. Although we were not able to see our friends, the Ummels, we did get to have dinner with Mike and Willie Munson from Arkansas. They lived in Colorado Springs in the past where we met. Our main reason for visiting Branson was to see the show "Queen Esther" at the Sight and Sound Theater. We were absolutely blown away by this excellent story with the theme, "You have been born for such a time as this." Queen Esther remained faithful to her God and was rewarded for her decision. The stage set-up was incredible to support a fabulous story.

In addition to seeing Queen Esther, we also saw "The Shepherd's Carol," a modern-day version of the story of Scrooge. This show was well worth the effort, reminding us of the importance of treating other people well and enjoying the life God has given you. Another highlight was seeing a show by the Duttons. They are a talented family whose children and grandchildren each play numerous different instruments and deliver a very wholesome show. In my mind, their talent and show are equivalent to the productions of the Sight and Sound Theater. It is definitely a show worth your time and money. They have the best violinist, guitarist and veteran's presentation in Branson. We also took in the show, Country Jubilee, which was filled with comedy but not on the scale of the other shows.

We stayed at the Surrey Crowne Grand Resort, which was very nice, with a Kitchen and living room. It also has a large pool, hot tub and fitness center we enjoyed. Right next to our resort was the Thousand Hills Golf Course and we played 18 holes of golf. It is featured as the best golf course in Branson. We were able to rent clubs for $15 each, which was a nice discount. The only challenge we had was the weather was so cold and windy we postponed our play one day. There was a one-hour frost delay, but we were still able to get on the course by 10:30 am. While waiting to get on the course, we bought some warm golf gloves for both hands. We were so impressed with them that we bought John Plessinger, our golf buddy, and our three son-in-laws warm golf gloves for Christmas. Although this was a very challenging course being built on hills with lots of sand traps and ravines, we both did quite well and felt good about our progress in golf. We told our golf instructor, Chad, that he had taught us well.

Our greatest challenge on this trip was the long, 18 hour travel days traveling from Denver to Springfield, MO. We had a 2 ½ hour layover in Atlanta both ways. Having to catch an 8 am flight out of Denver made it a tiring day, but we survived. All four planes that we flew in were fully packed, which made flying more exhausting. But all in all, the trip to Branson was well worth all the time and effort I put into the preparation as a "travel agent."

Major Snow Storm
In the Rockies

On Wednesday, March 12, 2024, the weather forecasters were predicting a major rain and snowstorm to hit Colorado beginning March 13-15. Normally, the weather forecasters will share that a snow storm is likely overnight and maybe continuing through the next day but never lingering for 48 hours. But this is springtime in the Rockies, and any weather formation is possible. Only three weeks ago, we had three different fires in Colorado Springs. Two were on the Army base, Fort Carson, and one was at the Air Force Academy which has 28,000 acres in the forest. Fortunately, all three fires were contained very quickly, but it was a reminder that we live in an area that is highly susceptible to wildfires that can destroy property and homes. In 2012, the Waldo Canyon fire destroyed over 400 homes as the wind whipped up and became dangerous. Two years later, the Black Forest fire destroyed over 300 homes very quickly.

But on March 13, it was not a fire that was causing concern but the extreme amount of snow that was predicted in Colorado Springs. When Marsha and I woke up on March 14, there was ten inches of snow in our yard, and it was still lightly snowing. We were fortunate to have a neighbor in a cul-de-sac a few houses away who loves shoveling snow for many of his neighbors. We call him the "snow angel" as he normally gets up at 4 am, and instead of running for an hour, he will shovel snow for 4-5 homes. He enjoys getting his exercise and helping us out at the same time. What a wonderful gift he is to many of us seniors.

My wife and I volunteered to help our oldest daughter, Jewel, shovel snow, who lives 2 ½ miles from us. The problem is she lives up the hill from us and her road had not been snow plowed. This meant that we might not be able to get up there, plus she did not want us to be challenged with her long driveway. She had a small snow blower, but the snow was so high on her driveway, 18 inches, that her snow blower would not work. She had to remove a foot from the top before her machine would function. So she shoveled the top layer first and then used her snow blower to accomplish the task. Because her husband was in Chicago for work, she was left to do this monumental project. But persistence paid off and she cleared a path for a single car on the long driveway.

Since Marsha and I did not go help her, we decided to clear off the side and back patio of our home. By now, there was close to a foot of snow. For the next hour, we literally cleared all the snow on the side path, all the snow on the large patio (12x30 feet), and the cover of our spa (8x8 feet). This whole project gave us a great workout, and we both wore back braces to protect our backs. This whole time, we were moving the snow from the patio onto the grass next to the patio. This action would help the grass to get plenty of water in the winter/spring months when the snow melts. Hopefully, this would help to prevent winter kill from lack of moisture. This is one of the great challenges in having a lawn in Colorado. "Winter kill" means patches of your grass might not survive during the winter months and means you have to plant new grass in the spring.

Not only did March 13-14 bring us a snowstorm of ten inches, but after a short break, another snowstorm started at 5 pm on March 14 and snowed throughout the night. When we woke up on March 15, we were shocked to discover that the new storm had delivered 12 inches more than we had cleared the day before. This was unusual for freak snow storms to be that close together. So, we called our daughter up on the hill to see if she needed help. Fortunately, it only snowed eight inches at her home so she was able to use her snow blower and clear a path on her long driveway. Jewel gets the award for tenacity in getting the job done!

Since my wife and I did not help Jewel, we decided to get our snow clothes and boots on and shovel our own driveway. Yesterday, I put on my snow boots I got when I was stationed at Thule, Greenland over Easter which was absolutely critical to wear when the wind chill got down to minus 70 degrees. They are specifically designed for severe cold weather and have excellent rubber grips on the bottom for the ice and snow. It was great to put them to good use again. After 45 minutes of shoveling, the snow angel came by to give us a hand. We had it almost done but he helped us finish the job.

Then we told our other daughter, Chanelle, who only lives five houses up the street, that we would help her shovel her sidewalk and driveway. After helping Chanelle do her driveway for another 45 minutes, the "snow angel" came and helped us finish the job. It was now time to go home and see how we felt. Both of us still had energy left in our tank so we decided to clear the snow from the side and back patio as we had done yesterday. We were so glad that we had cleared the snow off this area yesterday, or it would have been twice as deep and much harder to clear. After another hour of shoveling the snow from the side of the garage and our large patio and spa cover, we finally decided to call it quits. We were tired and had met our match. We figured we had done 2 ½ hours of snow shoveling from 10 am to 12:30 pm. When we finished we both agreed that we were glad we had done it and we won't have to do it tomorrow. Not too bad for a young couple who are 76 and 75 years old. Just another day in paradise!!

Cruise Trip to the Southern Caribbean

This adventure was inspired by my first visit to Antigua back in 1989. I was a chaplain in the Air Force, stationed with the 302nd Flying Squadron at Peterson Air Force Base in

Colorado Springs, Colorado. Since I wasn't pastoring a church at the time, I had more opportunities to support the squadron. The Commander wanted me to fly with his troops as much as possible, which was a dream come true since I needed the income and loved flying.

One memorable mission took us to Antigua to support paratroopers testing night jumps into the waters around the island. After waking up at 3 am for the exercise, the rest of the day was free to explore. I swam in pristine waters, relaxed on white sandy beaches, and went snorkeling on a boat trip. This incredible experience made me dream of someday bringing my wife, Marsha, to Antigua. It took 35 years, but we finally made it happen.

Our dream trip was a 10-day cruise from April 29 to May 10, 2024. We flew from Denver to Fort Lauderdale the day before the cruise to ensure we didn't miss the ship. The flight was smooth, and I complimented the Captain, who graciously credited a young female pilot. The next day, we took a shuttle to Cape Canaveral, where the Emerald Princess was docked. The boarding process was quick and efficient, and we were on the ship by 11 am.

The ship used a medallion system for purchases and access, which was very convenient. For dinner, we chose open seating, allowing us to meet new people from all over the world. We left Fort Lauderdale at 3 pm, and the ocean was incredibly calm throughout our journey.

Our first day at sea allowed us to relax and catch up on sleep. I also joined a dance exercise class for some cardio. On day three, we visited Princess Cay, a private island. Despite some shuttle issues, we enjoyed a delicious barbecue lunch and a relaxing day on the beach.

In Saint Thomas, we took a gondola ride for a breathtaking view of the island. In Saint Martin, we explored both the French and Dutch sides on a bus tour. Saint John's, Antigua, brought back fond memories as we cruised around the island on a catamaran, snorkeled, and shopped for souvenirs.

In Saint Kitts, we encountered many vendors but enjoyed shopping and exploring the island. Tortola, known for its dark rum, was our last island stop. We finished our shopping and enjoyed the friendly locals and beautiful weather.

The last two days at sea were filled with delicious food, entertaining shows, and relaxing in our quiet balcony room with stunning ocean views. The whole cruise was a dream come true, and Marsha and I cherished every moment together.

Some Final Thoughts

When I began writing this memoir a few years ago, it was intended just for my family and close friends. I never thought I would publish it. But as time went on, it felt right to share these words with you, my dear readers. My hope is that as you journey through these chapters, you will find the same encouragement and strength I found in my own life. We all face challenging times—financial struggles, health issues, broken relationships, job losses, and unexpected events. Yet, with God's help, these tough moments can transform into opportunities and bring blessings into our lives.

One of the most important lessons I learned is to seek the silver lining in every storm. How we respond to life's events shapes our journey. Another key lesson is the power of gratitude.

Expressing thanks to God and others takes little effort but brings remarkable rewards. I am drawn to people who are grateful, as their presence is a gift. When you are around those who lack gratitude, something essential is missing from life. I am deeply thankful to you for taking the time to read my book. May you discover the joy and art of saying "Thank You." Your life will be enriched as you embrace a spirit of thankfulness.

Finally, my faith in a loving, personal, and infinite God has been my foundation. Without this belief, my life would not be complete. I warmly invite you to explore what it means to be a person of faith through all the highs and lows of life. I wish you nothing but the best on your journey.

To God be the Glory!

About the Author

Dave Markwalder is a loving husband, father of three daughters and four granddaughters. He is a retired Presbyterian minister of 42 years and served as an Air Force chaplain for 26 of those years. Dave had the privilege of recruiting scores of chaplains to shape the future of the US Air Force chaplaincy. Besides his Bachelor of Science degree, Dave has three master degrees and a Doctorate. He enjoys golfing, reading, traveling, hiking and playing the guitar. Although Dave has served or traveled on six of seven continents, his greatest joy is spending time with his family. He recently experienced a healing miracle in his brain that has extended his quality of life.

Made in United States
Troutdale, OR
03/11/2025

29674725R00142